Lecture Notes of the Institute for Computer Sciences, Social Informatics and Telecommunications Engineering   477

The LNICST series publishes ICST's conferences, symposia and workshops. It reports state-of-the-art results in areas related to the scope of the Institute.

LNICST reports state-of-the-art results in areas related to the scope of the Institute. The type of material published includes

- Proceedings (published in time for the respective event)
- Other edited monographs (such as project reports or invited volumes)

LNICST topics span the following areas:

- General Computer Science
- E-Economy
- E-Medicine
- Knowledge Management
- Multimedia
- Operations, Management and Policy
- Social Informatics
- Systems

Yasushi Kambayashi · Ngoc Thanh Nguyen ·
Shu-Heng Chen · Petre Dini · Munehiro Takimoto
Editors

Artificial Intelligence for Communications and Networks

4th EAI International Conference, AICON 2022
Hiroshima, Japan, November 30 – December 1, 2022
Proceedings

 Springer

Editors
Yasushi Kambayashi
Nippon Institute of Technology
Saitama, Japan

Shu-Heng Chen
National Chengchi University
Taipei, Taiwan

Munehiro Takimoto
Tokyo University of Science
Noda, Japan

Ngoc Thanh Nguyen
Wroclaw University of Science
and Technology
Wrocław, Poland

Petre Dini
IARIA
Wilmington, DE, USA

ISSN 1867-8211 ISSN 1867-822X (electronic)
Lecture Notes of the Institute for Computer Sciences, Social Informatics
and Telecommunications Engineering
ISBN 978-3-031-29125-8 ISBN 978-3-031-29126-5 (eBook)
https://doi.org/10.1007/978-3-031-29126-5

This Springer imprint is published by the registered company Springer Nature Switzerland AG
The registered company address is: Gewerbestrasse 11, 6330 Cham, Switzerland

Preface

We are delighted to introduce the proceedings of the fourth edition of the 2022 European Alliance for Innovation (EAI) International Conference on Artificial Intelligence for Communications and Networks (AICON 2022), held in Hiroshima, Japan, on November 30 and December 1, 2022. Following the successes of the first AICON (2019) in Harbin, China, the second AICON (2020) in virtual mode, and the third AICON (2021) in Xining, China, this conference continued to provide an internationally respected forum for scientific research into artificial intelligence and communication systems, and their applications. We received 36 submissions from which 9 full papers and 4 short papers were selected. We would like to mention a few notables amongst them.

Recent developments in Artificial Intelligence (AI) and Machine Learning (ML), especially in reinforcement learning and deep learning, have stimulated growing interests in incorporating AI and ML into communication systems and networks. Some researchers have advocated applying ML to communication system design. Based on this line, we had a session AI and Networks. In the session, a group from Carleton University proposed a heuristic algorithm that deals with a network virtualization problem, and a group from the Tokyo University of Science proposed a lightweight distributed reinforcement learning method that allows IoT devices to make appropriate parameter selections without requiring any prior information.

ML is now a mainstream of AI research, and we had two sessions with this theme. In the sessions, a group from the National Defense Academy proposed a learning model based on the bias and rising threshold algorithm in multi-agent reinforcement learning, a group from Japan Advanced Institute of Science and Technology demonstrated that a combination of one of the reinforcement learning methods and a task-conditioned reasoning strategy is effective. Another group from National Defense Academy proposed a model based on neural networks using human cognitive bias. Another group from Tokyo University of Science reported their development of a method for estimating the location of animals using a ML model. A joint group from Nippon Institute of Technology and Yamaguchi University proposed using an adaptive moment estimation optimization method for the fine-tuning process of a deep belief network. A group from the National Institution for Academic Degrees and Quality Enhancement of Higher Education reported their experiences constructing a course classification support system using deep learning that evaluates university syllabi.

Evolutionary computation is yet another mainstream of AI research. We had a proposal of a discrete mathematical model for seasonal influenza, and a utilization of the blockchain mechanism for the population-based optimization system to make a trust management system. We even had a proposal of a combination of the traditional logic-based AI methodology and evolutionary computation.

We had a successful panel discussion in a hybrid style around the globe. The moderator Steve Chan took control from the US. Eugen Borcoci participated from Romania and Petre Dini from the US. In addition to these remote participants, Takashi Kuremoto,

Hayato Ohwada and Atsushi Togashi participated in the discussion from the conference site. They provided a fruitful discussion about the theme new trends on artificial intelligence. The general chair deeply appreciated the commitment of the remote participants, when the panel discussion took place it was very late at night in the US and European time zones.

Many people contributed toward the success of the conference. First, we would like to recognize the local chair Saori Iwanaga from Japan Coast Guard Academy who dealt with all the hard work. Without her, we could not have organized this conference. We appreciate all the members of program committee for their dedication to the paper review. They ensured the high quality review process.

Our special thanks are due to Springer for publication of the proceedings and for its kind support.

Finally, we hope that AICON 2022 contributed significantly to the academic and practical excellence of the field and will lead to even greater success of AICON events in the future.

December 2022

Yasushi Kambayashi
Ngoc Thanh Nguyen
Shu-Heng Chen
Petre Dini
Munehiro Takimoto

Organization

Steering Committee

Imrich Chlamtac   University of Trento, Italy

Organizing Committee

General Chair

Yasushi Kambayashi   Nippon Institute of Technology, Japan

General Co-Chair

Petre Dini   International Academy, Research, and Industry Association, USA

TPC Chairs

Ngoc Thanh Nguyen   Wroclaw University of Science and Technology, Poland

Shu-Heng Chen   National Chengchi University, Taiwan

TPC Co-Chair

Munehiro Takimoto   Tokyo University of Science, Japan

Sponsorship and Exhibit Chair

Tsutomu Kumazawa   Software Research Associates, Inc, Japan

Local Chair

Saori Iwanaga   Japan Coast Guard Academy, Japan

Workshops Chair

Munehiro Takimoto   Tokyo University of Science, Japan

Publicity and Social Media Chair

Wei Shi   Carleton University, Canada

Publications Chair

Tomofumi Matsuzawa   Tokyo University of Science, Japan

Web Chair

Yasushi Kodama   Hosei University, Japan

Posters and PhD Track Chair

Takako Nakatani   The Open University of Japan, Japan

Panels Chair

Petre Dini   International Academy, Research, and Industry
                                 Association, USA

Technical Program Committee

Saori Iwanaga	Japan Coast Guard Academy, Japan
Tsutomu Kumazawa	Software Research Associates, Inc, Japan
Munehiro Takimoto	Tokyo University of Science, Japan
Yasushi Kodama	Hosei University, Japan
Kazuteru Miyazaki	National Institution for Academic Degrees and Quality Enhancement of Higher Education, Japan
Satoshi Tojo	Japan Advanced Institute of Scienece and Technology, Japan
Hiroki Suguri	Miyagi University, Japan
Tomofumi Matsuzawa	Tokyo University of Science, Japan
Shohei Taga	Tokyo University of Science, Japan
Takako Nakatani	The Open University of Japan, Japan

Takashi Kuremoto	Nippon Institute of Technology, Japan
Nobuhiko Itoh	Nippon Institute of Technology, Japan
Toshiyasu Kato	Nippon Institute of Technology, Japan
Kazuaki Rokusawa	Chiba Institute of Technology, Japan
Hiroshi Sato	National Defense Academy, Japan
Masaru Kamada	Ibaraki University, Japan
Satoshi Kodama	International Professional University of Technology in Tokyo, Japan
Kengo Morohashi	Chitose Institute of Science and Technology, Japan
Hiroki Kozu	Nippon Institute of Technology, Japan
Miho Nishizaki	Iwate Prefectural University, Japan
Hidefumi Ohmura	Tokyo University of Science, Japan
Trang Phan	Yeungnam University, Korea
Van Tham Nguyen	Thuyloi University, Vietnam
Wei Shi	Carleton University, Canada
Taesu Cheong	Korea University, Korea
Tetsuya Suzuki	Shibaura Institute of Technology, Japan
Masahide Yuasa	Shonan Institute of Technology, Japan
Sung-Bae Cho	Yonsei University, Korea
Yoshiaki Yasumura	Shibaura Institute of Technology, Japan
Masanori Goka	Fukuyama University, Japan
Kazuhiko Fukui	National Institute of Advanced Industrial Science and Technology, Japan
Kengo Fujisawa	Tokyo University of Science, Japan
Hiroyuki Takada	Nagasaki University, Japan
Hiroshi Yabe	Tokyo University of Science, Japan
Atsushi Suenaga	Nihon University, Japan
Christos Troussas	University of West Attica, Greece
Mianxiong Dong	Muroran Institute of Technology, Japan
Rosario Catelli	Institute for High Performance Computing and Networking – National Research Council, Italy
Pascal Lorenz	University of Haute Alsace, France

Contents

Evolutionary Computation

AI and Networks

Cost-Aware Node Ranking Algorithm
for Embedding Virtual Networks
in Internet of Vehicles

Khoa Nguyen$^{(\boxtimes)}$, Wei Shi , and Marc St-Hilaire

School of Information Technology, Carleton Univeristy, Ottawa, ON, Canada
{khoatnguyen,wei.shi,marc.sthilaire}@carleton.ca

Abstract. Internet of Vehicles (IoV), a subset of the Internet of Things (IoT), has been commonly considered as a primary paradigm for the anticipated success of the intelligent transportation. Network Virtualization (NV) enables flexible, cost-effective and on-demand services over the deployments of heterogeneous network service requests on a shared physical infrastructure. The most challenging problem of NV is Virtual Network Embedding (VNE) which involves embedding Virtual Network Requests (VNRs) into the substrate network efficiently and effectively, meeting several rigid resource constraints. In fact, the conventional VNE problem has been extensively investigated in the datacenter architecture in which the network topology is always fixed. Although recent studies have addressed the VNE problem considering IoV demands in datacenter networks, the development of VNE in IoV contexts, where connected and autonomous vehicles operate as substrate network nodes to handle incoming VNRs, is still in its early stages. This paper proposes a dual ranking-value and cost-aware heuristic algorithm, called CARA, for dealing with the online VNE problem in IoV. By considering vehicle mobility, our solution guarantees that the selected vehicles will remain within the preferable radius of the VNR while serving it. A thorough evaluation of our proposed VNE algorithm under the Random Waypoint (RWP) mobility model reveals that it accepts more than 40% VNRs while maintaining a drop-out ratio of almost zero and an execution time that is very practical.

Keywords: Network virtualization · Virtual network embedding · Vehicle ranking · Internet of vehicles · Heuristic algorithm

1 Introduction

Due to mobile traffic explosion, the growth of safety data, and the variety of vehicular applications in the field of intelligent transportation, extensive research on the Internet of Vehicles (IoV) becomes increasingly critical. In fact, connected vehicles and mobile infrastructure (e.g., roadside units, base stations) aren't always able to communicate with each other directly; thus, they will forward and receive messages/data through intermediate vehicles, forming irregular

© ICST Institute for Computer Sciences, Social Informatics and Telecommunications Engineering 2023
Published by Springer Nature Switzerland AG 2023. All Rights Reserved
Y. Kambayashi et al. (Eds.): AICON 2022, LNICST 477, pp. 3–19, 2023.
https://doi.org/10.1007/978-3-031-29126-5_1

self-organizing networks. In addition, migrating the computations from the core
network to the edge can reduce the network loads of the core network, especially during the peak hours. Virtual Network Embedding (VNE) can become a
propitious key for tackling the resource allocation problem in IoV. VNE enables
the physical network resources to be shared between different Virtual Network
Requests (VNRs) while maintaining an isolated coexistence of Virtual Networks
(VNs) on the underlying Substrate Network (SN).

The VNE problem has been widely acknowledged as $\mathcal{NP}$-Hard either for Virtual Node Mapping (VNoM) or Virtual Link Mapping (VLiM) [1,2]. Although a
number of optimization models (e.g., Integer Programming (IP)) are formulated
to approach optimal VNE solutions, they are not likely to be deployed for solving online VNE problems due to scalability, time complexity, and impractical
implementation issues. As a result, most VNE solutions focus on the efficient
design of heuristic algorithms to deal with the impediments of the formulated
optimization models. A typical VNE process comprises two stages: VNoM and
VLiM. Most VNE approaches have attempted to address the VNoM phase followed by the VLiM phase which usually relies on the shortest path methods
(e.g., Dijkstra's algorithm).

The VNE problem has been significantly studied in cloud computing in which
the network topology is always fixed. Therefore, conventional VNE approaches
cannot be used for IoV environments where vehicles move on roads dynamically and their locations keep changing over time. Vehicle communications is
indeed based on wireless links (e.g., IEEE 802.11p standard), and the eligible
vehicles from different vendors (e.g., Aspark, Apple, Audi, Tesla, Vinfast) can
practically register with service providers to provide network services. When a
VNR arrives and stays in the network for a random duration, it requires a particular topology with stringent network resources while the substrate topology
keeps changing over time due to vehicle mobility. This dynamism complicates
the design of VNE algorithms, and existing VNE approaches have not considered all these characteristics. Consequently, typical VNE approaches that work
efficiently under static network topologies might not work in IoV environments
since vehicles serving as service nodes are always changing their geographical
locations due to their mobility. Thus, VNE algorithms should be sufficiently fast
and should also consider vehicle mobility; otherwise, it could result in situations
where some of the selected vehicles are no longer able to provide the requested
services since they moved out of the preferable radius of the given VNR. Hence,
we need new VNE algorithms that can handle online VNRs in IoV environments.

In this paper, we propose a dual ranking-value and cost heuristic algorithm,
called CARA, for addressing the online VNE problem in IoV. The algorithm is
aimed at dual objectives in which the vehicles that obtained the highest ranking values while producing the lowest costs are rapidly selected for mapping the
VNR. First, it effectively ranks available vehicles based on network attributes,
and then the vehicle producing the lowest cost value among a proportional number of the best ranked vehicles is greedily selected for mapping the virtual node.
In fact, splittable mapping might theoretically support a better resource uti-

lization solution, but this approach could create abundant overheads through maintaining the consistency of the network state. Moreover, splittable embedding can lead to out-of-order deliveries which increases latency and becomes detrimental to delay-sensitive applications [3]. As a result, we merely consider unsplittable embedding solutions in this research. To the best of our knowledge, this is one of the very first papers that directly deals with the online VNE problem in IoV environments considering vehicle mobility. The major contributions of this paper can be summarized as follows:

- We study a centralized VNE model addressing the online VNE problem in IoV environments. Service time of vehicles, wireless communication links, vehicle locations and memory capacity are considered along with other typical resource constraints (e.g., CPU).
- We introduce a neighboring time factor to track the eligible vehicles for VNoM. This ensures that the selected vehicles will remain within the preferable radius of the VNR while serving it. Accordingly, we introduce three new performance metrics to testify this neighboring time: average initial acceptance ratio, actual acceptance ratio, and drop-out ratio. By introducing this neighboring time factor, we can remove a strong assumption that nodes remain available for the duration of the request, which is commonly used in most VNE papers.
- We propose an efficient heuristic VNE algorithm, called CARA, that ranks the available vehicles based on network attributes. The top ranked vehicles, driven by a cost function, form the best solution for mapping the corresponding virtual node. This cost function not only takes the cost of the preceding node mapping into account, but also considers those of all already-mapped node mappings to pre-minimize the cost values. By considering mapping cost in VNoM, it allows the solution to coordinate the link mapping in advance.
- We perform extensive evaluations under the Random Waypoint (RWP) mobility model. Our results indicate that the proposed algorithm performs better than five existing VNE algorithms, and it is also highly practical due to its fast execution time.

The remainder of this paper is organized as follows: the related work is presented in Sect. 2 while the network model is formulated in Sect. 3. Our proposed approach is described in Sect. 4. Performance evaluation is introduced in Sect. 5. Finally, Sect. 6 concludes the paper and presents future work.

2   Related Work

The VNE problem is commonly known as $\mathcal{NP}$-hard, which is intractable to solve by formulated optimization models due to high time complexity. Thus, the majority of the research papers in this field have focused on designing suboptimal heuristic algorithms.

Towards VNE research on conventional cloud computing, [2] proposed a node-link coordination relaxing the integer constraints for addressing the VNoM stage.

The rounding techniques were utilized to choose the most proper node mappings. Li et al. in [4] presented a VNE paradigm that jointly took both virtual resources and substrate resources of the core network into account in order to provide diversified services in 5G networks efficiently. Cao et al. in [5] and [6] introduced several network attributes and the global network resources for ranking substrate nodes and virtual nodes before mapping VNRs. Recently, [7] proposed three novel Genetic Algorithm (GA)-based approaches jointly coordinating virtual node and link mappings in a one-stage mapping where the VLiM stage was deployed on several different path searching methods. A novel conciliation mechanism was applied to deal with a set of infeasible link mappings in GA operations. Troia et al. in [8] proposed a VNE framework handling the admission control and resource allocation problems in 5G networks by deploying a deep reinforcement learning.

More specifically towards the VNE problem in IoV, the authors in [9] researched a bandwidth-aware VNE in multi-domain problems in the wireless communication mode. A Particle Swarm Optimization (PSO) algorithm was then introduced to enhance the performance of mapping VNRs. Recently, Fan et al. in [10] have investigated the hierarchy-based dynamic VNE problem in the static business environment considering IoV demands. The authors presented a node-evaluation model to sort and evaluate substrate nodes and then a global-resource capacity algorithm to solve the virtual node mappings.

However, all of those VNE papers merely concentrate upon addressing the VNE problem in conventional cloud computing scenarios. Even if [9] and [10] dealt with the VNE problem considering IoV requests in cloud computing, these papers are not solving the online VNE problem under IoV environments subject to vehicle movements. To the best of our knowledge, this is one of the very first papers tackling the online VNE problem directly, considering the vehicle mobility in IoV environment by a cost-aware vehicle ranking algorithm.

3   Network Model and Problem Description

3.1   Virtual Network Assignment

In this research, the software-defined edge computing paradigm in which the network is split into control plane and data plane is favored. The control plane is involved in the global view of the network while the data plane is related to the moving vehicles. Vehicles need to register with Service Providers (SPs) to provide network services, and periodically update their information to the controller such as state, location, velocity, and direction. With the aim of approaching a generic model for tackling the VNE problem in IoV environments, we model our network as a weighted undirected graph $G^s = (N^s, L^s)$, where N^s is a set of physical nodes (e.g., available vehicles) while L^s denotes the set of physical links. Vehicles can indirectly communicate with others via intermediate vehicles due to several issues such as blockages, security, capability, vendor preferences, etc. As a result, it is possible to have a physical path between a pair of vehicles that traverses several intermediate vehicles. A vehicular node $n^s \in N^s$ has multiple information

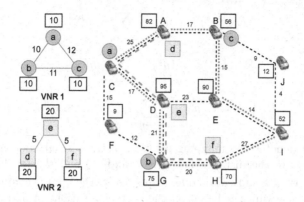

Fig. 1. An example embedding of VNRs onto a shared substrate network

including a current geographical location $loc(n^s)$ (i.e., GPS coordinates), the available CPU capacity $c(n^s)$, memory $m(n^s)$, and a registered service time $t_s(n^s)$ that the vehicle promises to deliver all assigned computational services while within the coverage of the corresponding base station at the registration. Furthermore, each vehicle also has a speed $s(n^s)$ and current direction $dir(n^s)$. On the other hand, each physical link $l^s \in L^s$ between a pair of vehicles possesses a $\zeta_s(l^s)$ link capacity. Without loss of generality, storage resources are excluded in this paper. Figure 1 shows a substrate network with two VNRs with node and link constraints. Similar to the substrate network, we model the ith arrived VNR as a weighted undirected graph denoted as $G_i^v = (N_i^v, L_i^v)$, where N_i^v expresses the set of virtual nodes and L_i^v denotes the set of corresponding virtual links. Each virtual node $n_i^v \in N_i^v$ requires a CPU capacity $c(n_i^v)$, memory $m(n_i^v)$, whereas each virtual link $l_i^v(s_i^v, d_i^v) \in L_i^v$ between a virtual source node s_i^v and a virtual destination node d_i^v has a demanded data rate capacity $b(l_i^v)$. Each VNR has a preferred mapping radius $D(n_i^v)$ which states how far the virtual node n_i^v can be allocated from $loc(n_i^v)$, and it also has a lifetime $t_v(G_i^v)$. Similar to many VNE research paper, our main objective is to maximize the average acceptance ratio which has been widely considered as the most important factor in VNE, accompanying with average revenue, average cost and average path length whilst meeting node and link constraints imposed by VNRs. Given the above notation, the node and link constraints can be formulated as follows:

Node constraints:

$$c(n_i^v) \le \mathcal{R}_{N_c}(E_N(n_i^v)) \tag{1}$$

$$m(n_i^v) \le \mathcal{R}_{N_m}(E_N(n_i^v)) \tag{2}$$

$$\mathcal{D}(loc(n_i^v), loc(E_N(n_i^v))) \le D(n_i^v) \tag{3}$$

$$t_v(G_i^v) \le \mathcal{R}_{t_s}(E_N(n_i^v)) \tag{4}$$

$$E_N(n_i^v) \in N^s \tag{5}$$

$$\mathcal{R}_{N_c}(n^s) = c(n^s) - \sum_{n_i^v \to n^s} c(n_i^v) \tag{6}$$

$$\mathcal{R}_{N_m}(n^s) = m(n^s) - \sum_{n_i^v \to n^s} m(n_i^v) \tag{7}$$

$$\mathcal{R}_{t_s}(n^s) = t_s(n^s) - \sum_{n_i^v \to n^s} t_v(G_i^v), n_i^v \in G_i^v \tag{8}$$

where $E_N(n_i^v)$ denotes the mapping solution of the virtual node n_i^v. $\mathcal{D}(i^s, j^d)$ and $\mathcal{R}_{N_{c|m}}(n^s)$ are the distance between i^s and j^d, and the residual CPU or memory capacity of a substrate node, respectively. $\mathcal{D}(i^s, j^d)$ is computed by the Euclidean distance which is based on the current locations of nodes i^s and j^d. In addition, $\mathcal{R}_{t_s}(n^s)$ denotes the remaining service time of vehicular node n^s. In VNE, a substrate node is only permitted to allocate to a virtual node in the given VNR.

Link constraints:

$$\zeta(l^s) = W log(1 + \gamma(l^s)) \tag{9}$$

$$\zeta(e^s) = \min_{l^s \in e^s} \zeta(l^s) \tag{10}$$

$$\zeta(e^s) \geq b(l_i^v), \forall e^s \in \mathcal{E}^s(E_L(l_i^v)) \tag{11}$$

$$0 \leq \zeta(l^s) \leq \zeta_s(l^s) \tag{12}$$

where $\mathcal{E}^s(E_L(l_i^v))$ denotes the set of all available paths from source $E_N(s_i^v)$ to destination node $E_N(d_i^v)$. $\gamma(l^s), \zeta(e^s)$ and W are the Signal to Interference and Noise Ratio (SINR) of the Vehicle-to-Vehicle (V2V) link l^s, the capacity of the path $e^s \in \mathcal{E}^s$ and channel bandwidth, respectively. To lessen the inter-system interference in massive multiuser Multiple-Input Multiple Output (MIMO) transmission environments, the zero-forcing pre-coder can be implemented to project the interference in the orthogonal space and gain high spectral efficiency of V2V links by re-utilizing the cellular spectrum [11]. To reflect the network loads, rather than being dependent on specific wireless technologies, each link capacity is configured as units varying in the specific range that can be easily converted to the real values. This is applicable to a generic model, and consistent with CPU and memory capacities. Considering that the channel state fluctuates during the embedding process, each substrate link capacity is randomly attenuated within $[0-\rho]$ subject to the distance between a pair of vehicles. An embedding solution is implied as feasible if and only if it satisfies the resource constraints (1–8) for node mapping or (9–12) for link mapping. Similar to most VNE approaches, the VNE algorithm in this work comprise two separate mapping stages for embedding a given VNR: VNoM followed by VLiM.

3.2 Performance Metrics

The most important objective when dealing with the VNE problem is to maximize the number of accepted VNRs along with optimizing the revenues and the corresponding mapping cost. In fact, these aforementioned metrics have been widely used to evaluate the efficiency of VNE algorithms. The revenue is the sum of the total virtual resources embedded on the SN over time, whereas the embedding cost of the ith VNR $C(G_i^v)$ is calculated as the sum of total substrate resources allocated to the ith VN.

Revenue ratio of ith VNR G_i^v can be formulated as:

$$\Xi(G_i^v) = w_b * \sum_{l_i^v \in L_i^v} b(l_i^v) + w_n * \sum_{n_i^v \in N_i^v} c(n_i^v) + w_m * \sum_{n_i^v \in N_i^v} m(n_i^v) \qquad (13)$$

Cost ratio of ith VNR G_i^v can be formulated as:

$$\Theta(G_i^v) = \sum_{n_i^v \in N_i^v} c(n_i^v) + \sum_{n_i^v \in N_i^v} m(n_i^v) + \sum_{l_i^v \in L_i^v} \sum_{l^s \in L^s} f_{l^s}^{l_i^v} \qquad (14)$$

where Ξ and Θ denote the generated revenue and network cost, respectively. $b(l_i^v)$ and $c(n_i^v)$ define the requested bandwidth of the virtual link l_i^v and the requested CPU of the virtual node n_i^v, whilst w_b, w_n and w_m are the unit weights of the bandwidth, CPU and memory resources, respectively. Likewise, $f_{l^s}^{l_i^v}$ defines the bandwidth of substrate link l^s that is allocated to the virtual link l_i^v. In this paper, we introduce three new metrics that are related to the number of accepted VNRs.

Initial Acceptance Ratio (IAR): defines a ratio between the number of accepted VNRs over the number of arrived VNRs during an interval time τ. IAR can be calculated as Eq. (15) below:

$$IAR = \left| \frac{\xi^a(\tau)}{\xi(\tau)} \right| \qquad (15)$$

where $\xi^a(\tau)$ and $\xi(\tau)$ are the number of the embedded VNRs and the total number of VNRs respectively.

Actual Acceptance ratio (AAR): defines a ratio between the number of accepted and successfully completed VNRs over the number of arrived VNRs during an interval time τ. This is different from the IAR as a request can be initially accepted but as nodes are moving, it may not be able to successfully complete the request. AAR can be computed using Eq. (16):

$$AAR = \left| \frac{\xi^{a_n}(\tau)}{\xi(\tau)} \right| \qquad (16)$$

where $\xi^{a_n}(\tau)$ is the number of the successfully embedded VNRs considering the neighboring time of the vehicles which is defined in Eq. 17 and 18.

$$\mathcal{T}_{\mathcal{NT}}(n^s) = \sum_{\kappa_i \in K_r} \frac{d_{\kappa_i}}{v_{\kappa_i}} \qquad (17)$$

$$\mathcal{T}_{\mathcal{NT}}(n^s) \geq t_v(G_i^v) \qquad (18)$$

where K_r is the number of trajectories of a vehicle when it reaches the border-line of the preferred radius of the VNR from its current location. K_r can be determined by the controller through communicating with vehicles while they are within its serving coverage.

Drop-out ratio (DR): defines a ratio between the differential number of the initial accepted VNRs and the successfully completed VNRs over the number of arrived VNRs during an interval time τ as calculated in Eq. (19):

$$DR = \left| \frac{\xi^a(\tau) - \xi^{a_n}(\tau)}{\xi(\tau)} \right| \tag{19}$$

4   Proposed Solution

This section presents a novel VNE algorithm consisting of three sub-stages: first the pre-processing stage chooses all available vehicles that meets the resource constraints including the neighboring time constraint to serve VNRs. Then, the vehicle ranking evaluates the selected vehicles from the previous stage by ranking them based on network attributes. Finally, a cost function is deployed to decide the vehicle that produces the lowest cost in a proportional number of the highest ranked-value vehicles for mapping the corresponding virtual node. Our approach handles a single virtual node at a time in the VNR until all virtual nodes are processed successfully. After achieving a mapping solution for all virtual nodes in a given VNR, the shortest path method is implemented for VLiM.

4.1   Pre-processing Stage

This operation is aimed at narrowing down the search space, in which the vehicles that satisfy several stringent resource constraints consisting of CPU, memory, service time, preferable radius of the VNR and the neighboring time as defined in Eqs. (17–18) are selected as potential node mappings. More precisely, vehicular nodes meeting Eqs. (1–8) are taken into account for mapping the virtual node. Vehicles must satisfy resource constraints demanded by the VNR, and their remaining service time must be long enough to provision services. Additionally, those vehicles must remain within the required radius of the VNR while serving it. Intuitively, vehicles that are closer to the source of the user request are more likely to be chosen for embedding the virtual node. At first glance, this strategy seems good enough for mapping a single virtual node. We also need to consider the vehicle's current speed and its direction to estimate the availability of the vehicle to ensure that the vehicle is always within the VNR's preferable radius while serving it. Otherwise, this can lead to a situation where the vehicle could move away from the radius of the request while providing its services, which would result in service disruption, allocated resource waste, and unexpected re-mappings. For this reason, existing VNE approaches are not well suited for IoV environments. To solve this problem, in this paper, we propose a function to estimate the remaining time that a vehicle is still within the VNR's preferable radius, called the neighboring time, to serve the given VNR.

Another challenge is that a VNR always includes a set of virtual nodes connected by virtual links to form a virtual network. Thus, the node mappings are admitted to create a considerable influence on the successive link mappings. Each node mapping does affect the successive embedding as well as the whole solution of the node mappings in general.

Suppose we have a set of eligible vehicles selected by the pre-processing stage that can allocate to a virtual node. We generally need to evaluate each vehicle in this set to decide the most appropriate one. Most of the recent VNE algorithms are using the node ranking approach to determine the importance of substrate nodes in a static topology based on network attributes, which attempt to exploit the possible relationships between these attributes and combine them in a single weighted formulation to recursively rank the nodes until obtaining a stable performance. These approaches are indeed inapplicable in IoV environments in which the network topology is extremely dynamic and the environment behaviors are nonstationary. Furthermore, finding out mutual relationships between different network attributes that possess very different characteristics and dimensions, and then combining them together are not indeed an easy task. Moreover, recent ranking approaches have not considered the embedding cost between the already-mapped nodes and each node in the set of potential nodes in order to select the best one. To solve this problem, we propose a ranking mechanism based on network attributes to rank the potential nodes determined from the pre-processing stage. A proportional number of the highest ranked vehicles are then chosen for the next stage where the most appropriate vehicle for mapping the virtual node is selected by the cost function. This cost function takes the cost of all already-mapped nodes into account and allows to directly coordinate the link mapping into the virtual node mapping in advance. Our solution can balance a trade-off between the vehicle producing a high ranked value while achieving a low embedding cost. Without considering the whole network topology, thanks to the pre-processing stage, our solution is not only scalable, but also adaptable to any sudden changes in the SN.

4.2   Vehicle Ranking

As described in the previous section, vehicle ranking will rank the available vehicles selected from the pre-processing stage based on network attributes. Instead of trying to obtain stable ranking values for all substrate nodes in a static SN, our approach simply needs to consider the previous node mappings, which allows to rapidly adapt to the uncertainty of vehicle mobility or scalability issues. The proposed VNE algorithm can quickly handle topology changes due to vehicle mobility, outage, exhausted lifetime, or any unexpected incidents. By taking all previous node mappings into account, the fragmentation problem can be reduced, improving the average acceptance ratio.

Node Degree defines the total number of adjacent edges of a node n^s in the network.

$$\Phi(n^s) = \sum_{m^s \in \nu_n} \sigma(l_{\overline{n^s m^s}}^s) \qquad (20)$$

where ν_n is a set of current neighbors of the vehicle n^s, and σ is a binary function that equals to 1 if there is a direct adjacent edge between n^s and m^s. Node degree, also acknowledged as degree centrality, implies connectivity, interaction, and the extensibility of a vehicular node. It indicates the capability to communicate with other vehicular nodes directly. A higher node degree is more favorable.

Node Intensity sums all adjacent link capacity of node n^s in the network.

$$I(n^s) = \sum_{m^s \in \nu_n} \zeta(l_{\overline{n^s m^s}}^s) \qquad (21)$$

The intensity attribute measures the strength of a vehicular node, which might have a big impact on the VLiM phase. Therefore, a high node intensity is more preferable.

Neighboring Distance defines the total distance of a node to all its neighbors. Vehicular nodes, that are closer to each other, can improve the resource fragmentation and somehow prevent service interruptions caused by uncertain vehicle mobility. Hence, smaller values of neighboring distance is desired.

$$\Pi(n^s) = \sum_{m^s \in \nu_n} \mathcal{D}(n^s, m^s) \qquad (22)$$

where

$$\mathcal{D}(n^s, m^s) = \sqrt{(x_{n^s} - x_{m^s})^2 + (y_{n^s} - y_{m^s})^2} \qquad (23)$$

Node Strength determines the total strength of a vehicular node considering the remaining resources such as CPU and memory, node degree and node intensity.

$$\mathcal{S}(n^s) = \mathcal{R}_{N_c}(n^s) * \mathcal{R}_{N_m}(n^s) * \Phi(n^s) * \frac{I(n^s)}{\Pi(n^s)} \qquad (24)$$

The normalized $\mathcal{S}$ is calculated as follows:

$$\overline{\mathcal{S}}(n^s) = \frac{\mathcal{S}(n^s)}{\sum_{n^s \in \mathcal{P}_v} \mathcal{S}(n^s)} \qquad (25)$$

where $\mathcal{P}_v$ denotes the set of vehicles selected from the pre-processing stage.

4.3   Intermediate Node Cost

Although vehicle ranking can evaluate the importance of a vehicular node, it does not reflect the interactions between the node and the already-mapped nodes of the VNR, and the embedding cost if the node is chosen considering the previous knowledge of node mappings. Hence, we introduce a new attribute, called intermediate node cost Ψ, to estimate the potential mapping cost if a node is selected for embedding the corresponding virtual node subject to all already-mapped nodes as calculated in Eq. (26).

$$\Psi(n^s) = c(n_i^v) + m(n_i^v) + \sum_{u^v k^v \in G_i^v} b(u^v k^v) * \Upsilon(e^s)),$$

$$\forall n^s \in E_N(u^v), n^s \in \mathcal{P}_v, \ k^v \in \mathcal{M}_a, \ e^s \in \mathcal{E}^s(E_L(u^v k^v)). \tag{26}$$

where $\Upsilon(e^s)$ denotes the hop-count of a substrate path e^s.

The normalized intermediate node cost is calculated as follows:

$$\overline{\Psi}(n^s) = \frac{\Psi(n^s)}{\displaystyle\sum_{n^s \in \mathcal{P}_e} \Psi(n^s)} \tag{27}$$

where $\mathcal{P}_e$ is the elite vehicles that are sorted out from $\mathcal{P}_v$. After ranking the nodes in the node ranking stage, a proportional number of elite vehicles obtaining the highest ranking values are selected for the next stage. The vehicle producing the lowest intermediate cost, calculated from Eq. (26), is then greedily preferred as the node mapping for the given virtual node. This approach does not only balance the trade-off between the ranking values and the embedding cost, but also simplifies the difficulty of integrating different domains of network attributes having different characteristics.

4.4   VNE-IoV Algorithm

Algorithm 1 illustrates our VNE solution, called **CARA**, in which the network input is the SN and a VNR as indicated in Line 2, whereas the output is the node and link mappings for the VNR. Our algorithm also adapts to this requirement. The proposed VNE algorithm begins with the node mapping stage in lines [5–19], followed by the link mapping phase in lines [20–23]. In terms of the node mapping, the pre-processing stage in lines [6–9] picks the available vehicles from the SN satisfying multiple resource constraints (Eqs. (1–8), (17), (18)) and adds to $\mathcal{P}_v$. Then the algorithm computes the normalized strength vector $\overline{S}$ for all vehicles in $\mathcal{P}_v$ through Eqs. (20–25) and sorts the vector $\overline{S}$ in descending order in lines [10–13]. Line 14 indicates that the proportional number of vehicles generating the highest ranking values are selected and then added to the elite set $\mathcal{P}_e$, where η denotes the candidate selection proportion. In lines [15–17], the algorithm calculates the normalized vector $\overline{\Psi}$ as Eqs. (26–27) and then selects the vehicle that produces the lowest cost value as the node mapping for the corresponding virtual node n_i^v in line 18. The VNoM is repeated until all virtual

---

Algorithm 1 : CARA

1: **Input**:
2:     Network G^s and VNR G_i^v
3: **Output**:
4:     The mapping solution for G_i^v.
    ▷ Virtual nodes and links in a given VNR are processed in order.
    ▷ Node Mapping:
5: **for** $n_i^v \in N_i^v$ **do**
    ▷   Pre-processing:
6:     **for** $n_s \in N_s$ **do**
7:         **if** n^s satisfies Eqs. (1)-(8), 17, 18 **add** n^s to $\mathcal{P}_v$
    ▷ $\mathcal{P}_v$ denotes a set of available vehicles after pre-processing stage.
8:     **end for**
9:     **if** $\mathcal{P}_v$ is empty **reject** the VNR.
    ▷   Vehicle Ranking:
10:     **for** $j \in |\mathcal{P}_v|$ **do**
11:         Calculate Eqs. (20)-(25) to achieve vector $\overline{\mathcal{S}}(\mathcal{P}_v[j])$
12:     **end for**
13:     Sort $\overline{\mathcal{S}}$ in descending order
14:     $\mathcal{P}_e \leftarrow \eta \times |\mathcal{P}_v|$ ▷ η: candidate selection proportion
    ▷   Intermediate node cost:
15:     **for** $k \in |\mathcal{P}_e|$ **do**
16:         Calculate Eqs. (26)-(27) to obtain vector $\overline{\Psi}(\mathcal{P}_e[k])$
17:     **end for**
18:     Select $\mathcal{P}_e[k]$ producing the smallest values of $\overline{\Psi}(\mathcal{P}_e[k])$
19: **end for**
    ▷ Link Mapping:
20: **for** $l_i^v \in L_i^v$ **do**
21:     Using the shortest path method to find the solution for l_i^v based on the information of achieved node mappings
22:     **if** l_i^v fails to map **reject** the VNR.
23: **end for**

---

nodes are successfully handled. The VLiM is conducted in lines [20–23] to embed each virtual link to a feasible path. If any node or link is unsuccessfully to map, the whole VNR will be rejected (lines (9), (22)).

5   Performance Evaluation

We compare our proposed algorithm against several VNE algorithms consisting of BEST_FIT, FIRST_FIT, RANDOM, G-SP [2] and ETAGNR [5]. For BEST_FIT, the virtual node will be allocated to the vehicle possessing the least available resources (e.g., CPU, memory) to meet the VNR [12], whereas FIRST_FIT picks the first vehicle in the substrate nodes that satisfies the resource constraints. In contrast, the RANDOM algorithm determines the available vehicle for virtual node mapping randomly. G-SP is broadly recognized as the most popular unsplittable VNE algorithm and also one of the fastest algorithms in this field, while ETAGNR exploits the topology attributes and the global network resources for ranking the substrate nodes.

Performance evaluations are divided into two parts. In the first part, we demonstrate the efficiency of our proposed cost-aware ranking algorithm by comparing the initial average acceptance ratio, average revenue, average cost, and average path length when processing VNRs at different traffic loads. In this evaluation, we remove the neighboring time from the proposed algorithm, called CARA_noNT, to justify the CARA algorithm itself. In the second part, we evaluate the effect of the neighboring time factor as described in Sect. 4.1. The neighboring time factor is evaluated by calculating the actual acceptance ratio and the drop out ratio. Furthermore, we also compare the average execution time between all algorithms at different network loads. Our simulation is conducted on a Ubuntu 22.04.1 LTS 64-bit platform with 16 GB memory and Intel Core i5-6200U CPU@2.30 GHz×4.

5.1 Simulation Setup

We have developed a discrete-event simulator to assess the proposed VNE algorithm and other rivals. The GT-ITM topology generator is utilized to create SN and VNs. SN has 50 nodes with 208 edges, and the physical CPU/link and memory capacities are uniformly distributed between [50–100] units and [100–200] units, respectively. The VNR arrivals follow the Poisson process with a mean arrival rate of λ requests per time unit, while their lifetime follows an exponential distribution with a mean $1/\mu = 1000$ time units. The miscellaneous loads of VNRs can be evaluated by $\lambda \times (1/\mu)$ Erlangs. Accordingly, the arrival rates of VNRs in this paper are varied between 1 and 8 requests per 100 time units. ρ and η are set out to 30% and 50%, respectively. With arbitrary SN and VNs generated for extensive evaluations, it indicates that our proposed algorithm can adapt to any topologies with diverse traffic patterns. Each simulation runs for 50,000 time units, which is 50 times longer than the average lifetime of a VN. This allows to generate a large number of independent samples. All performance figures were based upon average values with 95% confidence interval. The error bars are tiny due to the large number of samples used, which shows that our simulation results are reliable.

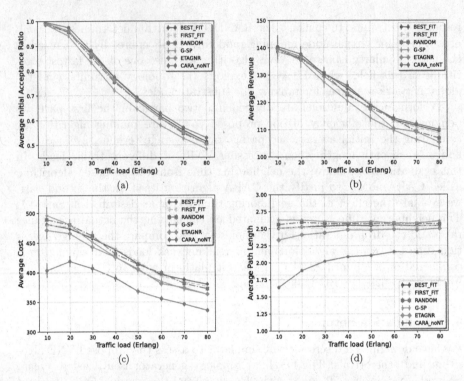

Fig. 2. (a) Average IAR (b) Average revenue (c) Average cost (d) Average path length

5.2 Vehicle Mobility Model

With the aim to approach a generic model for the VNE problem in IoV environments and to primarily concentrate on investigating the resource allocation, we used the Random Waypoint (RWP) model [13] to evaluate all VNE algorithms in this paper. Each vehicle randomly moves within a simulation area (1000×1000) with a random direction and a random speed in a range of $[5–60\,\text{km/h}]$, and the pausing time is set to 100 time units. We have used the BonnMotion software [14] to generate the vehicle mobility patterns under tracing files. When running simulations, the simulator reads the tracing files and updates the vehicles' information into the substrate network.

5.3 Evaluation Results

Performance results are illustrated in Figs. 2 and 3. For the first part of the evaluation, as we want to emphasize the efficiency of the proposed algorithm, we do not consider the neighboring time in the pre-processing stage. The proposed algorithm in this evaluation is called CARA_noNT. Figure 2a indicates that our algorithm accepts more VNRs than all rivals. The reason is that the proposed algorithm has an efficient cost-aware ranking mechanism with effective network

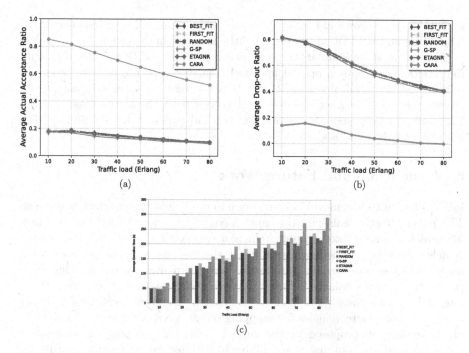

Fig. 3. (a) Average AAR (b) Average DR (c) Average execution time

attributes. Among the rivals, ETAGNR performs better than others when the traffic load is low, but when the traffic load increases, BEST_FIT, FIRST_FIT, and RANDOM perform better than ETAGNR while G-SP performs worst. Figures (2b–2c) confirm these results since CARA_noNT achieves the highest average revenue while producing the lowest average embedding cost. The results of Fig. 2c is validated by Fig. 2d when the proposed algorithm CARA_noNT obtains the shortest path length.

In the second part of the evaluation, we reevaluated the node mappings that are part of all VNE algorithms. If the vehicles selected by the algorithms moved away from the preferred mapping radius of the VNRs, they are marked as unsuccessful VNRs. In this evaluation, our proposed algorithm, called CARA, considers the neighboring time in the pre-processing stage. We compare the VNE algorithms towards the average actual acceptance ratio and the drop-out ratio. The results show that CARA significantly outperforms all other algorithms as its initial acceptance ratio (Fig. 2a) and its actual acceptance ratio (Fig. 3a) are relatively close. CARA with neighboring time consideration performs best among others, especially when the network becomes congested. As shown in Figs.(3a–3b), CARA keeps high acceptance ratios ranging from 52.82% to 85.64% while remaining the drop-out ratio almost zero at the highest traffic loads. In contrast, the initial acceptance ratios of the rivals in Fig. 2a are now significantly reduced from 39.52% up to 82% as illustrated through the average drop-out ratio in Fig. 3b, leading to their very low actual acceptance ratios varying from 9.1% up to only 18.7% as shown in Fig. 3a. All rivals perform quite similar in general, and BEST_FIT and RANDOM perform slightly better than the others in particular.

Finally, we also measured the execution time of all VNE algorithms to identify the practicality of our proposed approach. As shown in Fig. 3c, the execution time of the proposed algorithm (CARA) is competitive since it rapidly ranks the available vehicles that have been sorted out from the pre-processing stage. Therefore, the proposed VNE algorithm is not only efficient in embedding VNRs, but also practical and scalable.

6 Conclusion and Future Work

IoV is foreseen to become a major research in intelligent transportation systems. This paper directly deals with the online VNE problem in IoV environments taking vehicle mobility into account. Vehicular service time, wireless links, current vehicle locations, and memory capacity are also considered in the proposed VNE model. Furthermore, we also proposed a novel cost-ware vehicle-ranking algorithm that strikes a balance between the high ranking-values of vehicles and the interactions with already-mapped nodes through the intermediate cost to select the most appropriate vehicles for mapping online VNRs. Extensive simulations illustrate that our proposed VNE approach is not only efficient and scalable in the VN embedding, but also practical due to its rapid execution time. For future work, we plan to investigate extra mobility-related metrics and also to evaluate the proposed solutions under different mobility models.

References

1. Gil Herrera, J., Botero, J.F.: Resource allocation in NFV: a comprehensive survey. IEEE Trans. Netw. Serv. Manage. **13**(3), 518–532 (2016)
2. Chowdhury, M., Rahman, M.R., Boutaba, R.: Vineyard: virtual network embedding algorithms with coordinated node and link mapping. IEEE/ACM Trans. Netw. **20**(1), 206–219 (2012)
3. Paschos, G.S., Abdullah, M.A., Vassilaras, S.: Network slicing with splittable flows is hard. In: 2018 IEEE 29th Annual International Symposium on Personal, Indoor and Mobile Radio Communications (PIMRC), pp. 1788–1793 (2018)
4. Li, J., Zhang, N., Ye, Q., Shi, W., Zhuang, W., Shen, X.: Joint resource allocation and online virtual network embedding for 5G networks. In: 2017 IEEE Global Communications Conference (GLOBECOM 2017), pp. 1–6 (2017)
5. Cao, H., Yang, L., Zhu, H.: Embedding virtual networks using a novel node-ranking approach via exploiting topology attributes and global network resources. In: 2017 9th International Conference on Wireless Communications and Signal Processing (WCSP), pp. 1–6 (2017)
6. Cao, H., Yang, L., Zhu, H.: Novel node-ranking approach and multiple topology attributes-based embedding algorithm for single-domain virtual network embedding. IEEE Internet Things J. **5**(1), 108–120 (2018)
7. Nguyen, K., Huang, C.: Towards adaptive joint node and link mapping algorithms for embedding virtual networks: a conciliation strategy. In: IEEE Transactions on Network and Service Management, p. 1 (2022)

8. Troia, S., Vanegas, A.F.R., Zorello, L.M.M., Maier, G.: Admission control and virtual network embedding in 5G networks: a deep reinforcement-learning approach. IEEE Access **10**, 15860–15875 (2022)
9. Zhang, P., Wang, C., Aujla, G.S., Kumar, N., Guizani, M.: IoV scenario: implementation of a bandwidth aware algorithm in wireless network communication mode. IEEE Trans. Veh. Technol. **69**(12), 15774–15785 (2020)
10. Fan, W., et al.: Dynamic virtual network embedding of mobile cloud system based on global resources in internet of vehicles. IEEE Trans. Veh. Technol. **70**(8), 8161–8174 (2021)
11. Liu, X., Li, Y., Xiao, L., Wang, J.: Performance analysis and power control for multi-antenna V2V underlay massive MIMO. IEEE Trans. Wireless Commun. **17**(7), 4374–4387 (2018)
12. Light, J.: Green networking: a simulation of energy efficient methods. Procedia Comput. Sci. **171**, 1489–1497 (2020)
13. Kezia, M., Anusuya, K.V.: Mobility models for internet of vehicles: a survey. Wirel. Pers. Commun. **125**, 1857–1881 (2022). https://doi.org/10.1007/s11277-022-09637-7
14. Aschenbruck, N., Ernst, R., Gerhards-Padilla, E., Schwamborn, M.: Bonnmotion: a mobility scenario generation and analysis tool. In: ICST (2010)

Fault Diameter of Strong Product Graph of Two Paths

Yuxiang Yue[1,2(✉)] and Feng Li[1]

[1] College of Computer Science, Qinghai Normal University, Xining, China
yueyuxiang21@126.com
[2] The State Key Laboratory of Tibetan Intelligent Information Processing
and Application, Xining, China

Abstract. Strong product is an efficient method to construct large networks from small networks. Fault diameter is an important parameter to measure the fault tolerance and effectiveness of interconnection networks. In this paper, we first determine the vertex fault diameter of the strong product graph of two paths by constructing the internally vertex-disjoint paths between any two vertices in the graph, then we determine the edge fault diameter of the strong product graph of two paths by constructing the edge-disjoint paths between any two vertices in the graph. In addition, we propose an improved mesh network, whose model composed of strong product graph of two paths and has many excellent characteristics.

Keywords: Paths · Strong product graph · Vertex fault diameter · Edge fault diameter

1 Introduction

All graphs considered in this paper are simple and undirected graphs with neither loops nor multiple edges. Let G be a graph with vertex set $V(G)$ and edge set $E(G)$, we use $v(G)$ to denote the order of G. Let R be a path in G, the length of the path R is $v(R) - 1$ and denoted by $L(R)$. If G is a path, we denote it by P. Let x and y be any two vertices in G, we use (x, y) denotes the edge connects x and y. The length of the shortest path between x and y in G is called the distance between x and y, which is denoted by $d(G; x, y)$. Then the diameter of G is the maximum length of all distances between any two vertices in G, denoted by $d(G)$. The connectivity of G is the minimum cardinality of all vertex subsets in G which are deleted from G to obtain a unconnected or a trivial graph, denoted by $\kappa(G)$. Similarly, the edge connectivity of G is the minimum cardinality of all edge subsets in G which are deleted from G to obtain a unconnected or a trivial graph, denoted by $\lambda(G)$. We use $\delta(G)$ denote the minimum degree of G. A graph

Supported by the National Natural Science Foundation of China (11551002), and Natural Science Foundation of Qinghai Province (2019-ZJ-7093).

Y. Kambayashi et al. (Eds.): AICON 2022, LNICST 477, pp. 20–33, 2023.
https://doi.org/10.1007/978-3-031-29126-5_2

G is called maximally connected graph, if $\kappa(G) = \delta(G)$. We can get that a path P is a maximally connected graph with $\kappa(P) = \lambda(P) = \delta(P) = 1$. In addition, the definitions of strong product, vertex fault diameter and edge fault diameter are given below.

Definition 1. *Let* $G_1 = (V(G_1), E(G_1))$, $G_2 = (V(G_2), E(G_2))$, *the strong product of* G_1 *and* G_2 *is denoted by* $G_1 \boxtimes G_2$ *and the vertex set is* $V(G_1) \times V(G_2)$. *Any two distinct vertices* $x_1 y_1$ *and* $x_2 y_2$ *in* $G_1 \boxtimes G_2$ *are adjacent, if and only if* $x_1 = x_2$ *and* $(y_1, y_2) \in E(G_2)$, *or* $y_1 = y_2$ *and* $(x_1, x_2) \in E(G_1)$, *or* $(x_1, x_2) \in E(G_1)$ *and* $(y_1, y_2) \in E(G_2)$.

In this paper, we mainly consider such a class of strong product graph $P_m \boxtimes P_n$, where $P_m \boxtimes P_n$ denotes the strong product graph of a path with order $m \geq 2$ and a path with order $n \geq 2$. The strong product graph $P_3 \boxtimes P_7$ is shown on Fig. 1.

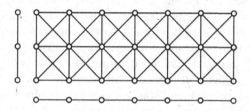

Fig. 1. The strong product graph $P_3 \boxtimes P_7$.

Definition 2. *Let* G *be a* w-*connected graph, and the faulty vertex set of* G *is denoted by* F *with* $|F| < w$. *The* $(w - 1)$-*vertex fault diameter of a graph* G *is defined as*

$$D_w(G) = max\{d(G - F) : F \subset V(G), |F| < w\}.$$

In the worst case, we can get $|F| = w - 1$. Therefore, for any w-connected graph G, the relation between diameter and vertex fault diameter holds

$$d(G) = D_1(G) \leq D_2(G) \leq \cdots \leq D_{w-1}(G) \leq D_w(G).$$

Definition 3. *Let* G *be a* t-*edge connected graph, and the faulty edge set of* G *is denoted by* F *with* $|F| < t$. *The* $(t - 1)$-*edge fault diameter of a graph* G *is defined as*

$$D'_t(G) = max\{d(G - F) : F \subset E(G), |F| < t\}.$$

In the worst case, we can get $|F| = t - 1$. Therefore, for any t-edge connected graph, the relation between diameter and edge fault diameter holds

$$d(G) = D'_1(G) \leq D'_2(G) \leq \cdots \leq D'_{t-1}(G) \leq D'_t(G).$$

The concept of strong product was first proposed in [1]. It is an efficient product method of constructing large graphs from small graphs, and the constructed strong product graphs retain many properties of subgraphs. Among them, there are many important results in the research on the connectivity and edge connectivity of strong product graphs. The lower bound of the connectivity of strong product graphs was first given in [2]. Then in [3], the edge connectivity of strong product graphs of two nontrivial connected graphs was determined, and the connectivity of strong product graphs of two maximally incomplete connected graphs was given. Later, the connectivity of strong product graphs was determined in [4]. There are also some recent results about product graphs in [5–7].

The topological structure of interconnection network is a graph, with its processors represented by vertices and links represented by edges. Especially, the diameter is used to indicate the transmission delay of interconnection network. In the network, if vertices or edges work for a long time, they will inevitably be faulty. After they are faulty, the information transmission of the network will be affected. Therefore, the network must have high fault tolerance and high effectiveness to reduce this impact as much as possible. The fault diameter is an important parameter to measure these properties, which includes vertex fault diameter and edge fault diameter. However, it is extremely difficult to determine the fault diameter in the actual network, so the compact upper bounds of the fault diameter of a general graph are given in [8,9]. But for some well-known networks, the fault diameter can be determined. The vertex fault diameters of kautz network and debrujin network are given in [10,11], the vertex fault diameters of pyramid network and star graph are determined in [12,13], and the edge fault diameter of hypercube network is given in [14]. There are also some recent results in [15,16].

Although many important results of the fault diameter of Cartesian product graphs are given in [17–19], for the fault diameter of strong product graphs, there are no relevant results. In this paper, we will start with a special class of strong product graph and give the determined vertex fault diameter and edge fault diameter. The vertex fault diameter of the strong product graph of two paths is first determined by constructing the internally vertex-disjoint paths between any two vertices in the graph, then we determine the edge fault diameter of the strong product graph of two paths by constructing the edge-disjoint paths between any two vertices in the graph. In addition, we propose an improved network model composed of the strong product graph of two paths, and compare it with the mesh network widely used in parallel computing systems.

2   Main Results

In order to prove the following results, we first specify the representation of the paths. Let $G = P_m \boxtimes P_n$, $x_h y_g$ and $x_p y_q$ are any two vertices in G, where $x_h, x_p \in V(P_m)$ and $y_g, y_q \in V(P_n)$. The path R_1 from vertex x_h to vertex x_p in P_m and its edge set is $E(R_1) = \{(x_i, x_{i+1}) : i = h, \cdots, p-1\}$, which can be expressed as $R_1 : x_h \to \cdots \to x_p$. The path R_2 from vertex y_g to vertex y_q in P_n and its edge set is $E(P_n) = \{(y_j, y_{j+1}) : j = g, \cdots, q-1\}$, which can be expressed as $R_2 : y_g \to \cdots \to y_q$. If $x_h = x_p$, then the path $x_h R_2$ connects vertex $x_h y_g$

and vertex $x_h y_q$ in G and its edge set is $E(x_h R_2) = \{(x_h, y_j) : j = g, \cdots, q-1\}$, which we express here as $x_h y_g \to \cdots \to x_h y_q$. Similarly, if $y_g = y_q$, then the path $R_1 y_g$ connects vertex $x_h y_g$ and vertex $x_p y_g$ in G and its edge set is $E(R_1 y_g) = \{(x_i, y_g) : i = h, \cdots, p-1\}$, which we express here as $x_h y_g \to \cdots \to x_p y_g$. If $x_h \neq x_p$ and $y_g \neq y_q$, then the path R_3 connects vertex $x_h y_g$ and vertex $x_p y_q$ in G and its edge set is $E(R_3) = \{(x_i, y_j) : i = h, \cdots, p-1, j = g, \cdots, q-1\}$, which we express here as $x_h y_g \to \cdots \to x_p y_q$. For convenience of expression, the path R_i can also be directly denoted by the label (i). For undefined symbols and terms, refer to [20].

The connectivity and diameter are the basic parameters necessary to discuss the vertex fault diameter of interconnection networks, we must first give the connectivity and diameter of the strong product graph of two paths. The following lemmas provide a solution.

Lemma 1 ([3]). *Let G_1 and G_2 be two maximally incomplete connected graphs with orders $n_1, n_2 \geq 2$, respectively. Then*

$$\kappa(G_1 \boxtimes G_2) = min\{\delta_1 n_2, \delta_2 n_1, \delta_1 + \delta_2 + \delta_1 \delta_2\}.$$

A path is a maximally connected graph. In particular, when the order is greater than 2, the path is a maximally incomplete connected graph.

Lemma 2. *Let P_m and P_n be two paths with orders $m, n \geq 2$, respectively. Then*

$$\kappa(P_m \boxtimes P_n) = \begin{cases} 2, & if \ m = 2, \ n > 2 \ or \ m > 2, \ n = 2, \\ 3, & otherwise. \end{cases}$$

Proof. Let $G = P_m \boxtimes P_n$ with $V(P_m) = \{x_1, \cdots, x_m\}$ and $V(P_n) = \{y_1, \cdots, y_n\}$, $x_h y_g$ and $x_p y_q$ are any two vertices in G, where $x_h, x_p \in V(P_m)$ and $y_g, y_q \in V(P_n)$. We discuss the following three cases.

Case 1. $m \geq 3, n \geq 3$. Since P_m and P_n are maximally incomplete connected graph, by Lemma 1, we have $\kappa(P_m \boxtimes P_n) = min\{m, n, 3\} = 3$.

Case 2. $m = 2, n = 2$. Since P_2 is a complete graph with order 2, we can get that $\kappa(P_2 \boxtimes P_2) = \kappa(K_2 \boxtimes K_2) = \kappa(K_4) = 3$.

Case 3. $m = 2, n > 2$ or $m > 2, n = 2$. Without loss of generality, we assume that $m > 2$ and $n = 2$, then $V(P_2) = \{y_g, y_q\}$. If we remove the vertex $x_{h+1} y_g$ and the vertex $x_{h+1} y_q$ from G, then we can get $G - \{x_{h+1} y_g, x_{h+1} y_q\}$ is not connected. Therefore, there have $\kappa(P_m \boxtimes P_2) \leq 2$. We consider the internally vertex-disjoint paths between any two vertices $x_h y_g$ and $x_p y_q$ in G. According to the positional relationship between the two vertices, it can be divided into the following three subcases.

Subcase 1. $x_h = x_p$. we can get that there are two internally vertex-disjoint paths R_1 and R_2 from $x_h y_g$ to $x_h y_q$ in G.

$$x_h y_g \to x_h y_q. \tag{1}$$

$$x_h y_g \to x_{h+1} y_g \to x_h y_q. \tag{2}$$

Subcase 2. $y_g = y_q$. we can get that there are two internally vertex-disjoint paths R_3 and R_4 from $x_h y_g$ to $x_p y_g$ in G.

$$x_h y_g \to \cdots \to x_p y_g. \tag{3}$$

$$x_h y_g \to x_{h+1} y_q \to \cdots \to x_{p-1} y_q \to x_p y_g. \tag{4}$$

Subcase 3. $x_h \neq x_p$ and $y_g \neq y_q$. we can get that there are two internally vertex-disjoint paths R_5 and R_6 from $x_h y_g$ to $x_p y_q$ in G.

$$x_h y_g \to \cdots \to x_{p-1} y_g \to x_p y_q. \tag{5}$$

$$x_h y_g \to x_{h+1} y_q \to \cdots \to x_p y_q. \tag{6}$$

There are always two internally vertex-disjoint paths from $x_h y_g$ to $x_p y_q$ in G. Therefore, there have $\kappa(P_m \boxtimes P_2) \geq 2$. We can get $\kappa(P_m \boxtimes P_2) = 2$. □

Lemma 3 ([20]). *Let $x_h y_g$ and $x_p y_q$ be any two vertices in strong product graph $G_1 \boxtimes G_2$, where $x_h, x_p \in V(G_1)$ and $y_g, y_q \in V(G_2)$. Then*

$$d(G_1 \boxtimes G_2; x_h y_g, x_p y_q) = \max\{d(G_1; x_h, x_p), d(G_2; y_g, y_q)\}.$$

Lemma 4. *Let P_m and P_n be two paths with orders $m, n \geq 2$, respectively. Then*

$$d(P_m \boxtimes P_n) = \max\{m, n\} - 1.$$

Proof. Let $G = P_m \boxtimes P_n$ with $V(P_m) = \{x_1, \cdots, x_m\}$ and $V(P_n) = \{y_1, \cdots, y_n\}$, $x_h y_g$ and $x_p y_q$ are any two vertices in G, where $x_h, x_p \in V(P_m)$ and $y_g, y_q \in V(P_n)$. By Lemma 3, we have

$$\begin{aligned} d(G; x_h y_g, x_p y_q) &= \max\{d(P_m; x_h, x_p), d(P_n; y_g, y_q)\} \\ &= \max\{|p - h|, |q - g|\} \\ &\leq \max\{m - 1, n - 1\} \\ &= \max\{m, n\} - 1. \end{aligned}$$

From the above formula, we can get that the distance between any two vertices in G is no more than $\max\{m, n\} - 1$. Therefore, we get the diameter of G is $\max\{m, n\} - 1$. □

Under the previous lemmas, we prove the following result by constructing the internally vertex-disjoint paths between any two vertices in the strong product graph of two paths.

Theorem 1. *Let P_m and P_n be two paths with orders $m, n \geq 2$, respectively. Then for any $1 \leq w \leq 3$, we have*

$$D_w(P_m \boxtimes P_n) = \begin{cases} \max\{m, n\} - 1, & for\ w = 1, \\ \max\{m, n\} - 1, & for\ w = 2\ and\ m \neq n\ or\ m = n = 2, \\ \max\{m, n\}, & for\ w = 2\ and\ m = n > 2, \\ \max\{m, n\}, & for\ w = 3\ and\ m \neq n\ or\ m = n > 3, \\ 1, & for\ w = 3\ and\ m = n = 2, \\ 4, & for\ w = 3\ and\ m = n = 3. \end{cases}$$

Proof. Let $G = P_m \boxtimes P_n$ with $V(P_m) = \{x_1, \cdots, x_m\}$ and $V(P_n) = \{y_1, \cdots, y_n\}$, $x_h y_g$ and $x_p y_q$ are any two vertices in G, where $x_h, x_p \in V(P_m)$ and $y_g, y_q \in V(P_n)$. Let F be the faulty vertex set of G with $|F| < w$.

By Lemma 2, we can get the connectivity of G. If only one of m and n is 2, $\kappa(G) = 2$, otherwise $\kappa(G) = 3$. By Lemma 4, we can get the diameter of G is $max\{m, n\} - 1$. For $w = 1$, there is no faulty vertex in F, we have $D_1(G) = d(G) = max\{m, n\} - 1$. Consider only $w > 1$, there are four cases that need to be discussed.

Case 1. $m = 2$, $n > 2$ or $m > 2$, $n = 2$. For any $1 \le w \le 2$, we have $G - F$ is connected. Without loss of generality, we assume that $m > 2$ and $n = 2$. The diameter of G is $m - 1 \ge 2$. By the Case 3 of Lemma 2, there are also three subcases.

Subcase 1. $x_h = x_p$. There are two internally vertex-disjoint paths R_1 and R_2 from $x_h y_g$ to $x_h y_q$ in G, we can get $L(R_1) = 1 < L(R_2) = 2 \le m - 1 = d(G)$. For $w = 2$, $|F| = 1$. Even in the worst case, we have $d(G - F; x_h y_g, x_h y_q) \le d(G)$.

Subcase 2. $y_g = y_q$. There are two shortest paths R_3 and R_4 whose interior vertices are disjoint from $x_h y_g$ to $x_p y_g$ in G, we can get $L(R_3) = L(R_4) = p - h \le m - 1 = d(G)$. For $w = 2$, $|F| = 1$. Even in the worst case, we have $d(G - F; x_h y_g, x_p y_g) \le d(G)$.

Subcase 3. $x_h \ne x_p$ and $y_g \ne y_q$. There are two shortest paths R_5 and R_6 whose interior vertices are disjoint from $x_h y_g$ to $x_p y_q$ in G, we can get $L(R_5) = L(R_6) = p - h \le m - 1 = d(G)$. For $w = 2$, $|F| = 1$. Even in the worst case, we have $d(G - F; x_h y_g, x_p y_q) \le d(G)$.

In this case, we can conclude that $D_2(G) \le d(G)$. For $1 \le w \le 2$, since $D_2(G) \ge d(G)$, we have $D_w(G) = d(G)$.

Case 2. $m = 2$, $n = 2$. For any $1 \le w \le 3$, we have $G - F$ is connected. Since $P_2 \boxtimes P_2 = K_4$, the diameter of G is 1. For $1 \le w \le 3$, $|F| = 2$. Even in the worst case, the two vertices $x_h y_g$ and $x_p y_q$ in G are still adjacent. Therefore, we can get $d(G - F; x_h y_g, x_p y_q) = 1 = d(G)$, such that $D_w(G) = d(G)$.

Case 3. $m > 3$, $n > 3$. For any $1 \le w \le 3$, we have $G - F$ is connected. The diameter of G is $max\{m, n\} - 1$. According to the positional relationship between the two any vertices $x_h y_g$ and $x_p y_q$ in G, we discuss the following two subcases.

Subcase 1. $x_h = x_p$ or $y_g = y_q$. Without loss of generality, we assume that $y_g = y_q$. According to the value range of g, there are two subcases.

Subsubcase 1. $g = 1$ or $g = n$. Without loss of generality, we assume that $g = 1$. Consider $p - h \ne 2$, we construct the internally vertex-disjoint paths which pass through all three neighbors of the vertex $x_h y_g$. For $w = 2$, $|F| = 1$. There are two shortest paths R_7 and R_8 whose interior vertices are disjoint from $x_h y_g$ to $x_p y_g$ in G.

$$x_h y_g \to x_{h+1} y_g \to \cdots \to x_{p-1} y_g \to x_p y_g, \tag{7}$$

$$x_h y_g \rightarrow x_{h+1} y_{g+1} \rightarrow \cdots \rightarrow x_{p-1} y_{g+1} \rightarrow x_p y_g, \tag{8}$$

with $L(R_7) = L(R_8) = p - h \leq m - 1 \leq max\{m, n\} - 1 = d(G)$. Even in the worst case, we have $d(G - F; x_h y_g, x_p y_g) \leq d(G)$. For $w = 3$, $|F| = 2$. There are three internally vertex-disjoint paths R_7, R_9 and R_{10} from $x_h y_g$ to $x_p y_g$ in G.

$$x_h y_g \rightarrow x_h y_{g+1} \rightarrow x_{h+1} y_{g+2} \rightarrow \cdots \rightarrow x_{p-2} y_{g+2} \rightarrow x_{p-1} y_{g+1} \rightarrow x_p y_g, \tag{9}$$

$$x_h y_g \rightarrow x_{h+1} y_{g+1} \rightarrow \cdots \rightarrow x_{p-2} y_{g+1} \rightarrow x_{p-1} y_{g+2} \rightarrow x_p y_{g+1} \rightarrow x_p y_g, \tag{10}$$

with $L(R_9) = L(R_{10}) = p - h + 1 \leq m \leq max\{m, n\} = d(G) + 1$. Even in the worst case, we have $d(G - F; x_h y_g, x_p y_g) \leq d(G) + 1$. There is also one special case where the previous method of constructing paths is not applicable. Consider $p - h = 2$, we construct three new internally vertex-disjoint paths R_{11}, R_{12} and R_{13} from $x_h y_g$ to $x_p y_g$ in G.

$$x_h y_g \rightarrow x_{h+1} y_g \rightarrow x_p y_g, \tag{11}$$

$$x_h y_g \rightarrow x_{h+1} y_{g+1} \rightarrow x_p y_g, \tag{12}$$

$$x_h y_g \rightarrow x_h y_{g+1} \rightarrow x_{h+1} y_{g+2} \rightarrow x_p y_{g+1} \rightarrow x_p y_g, \tag{13}$$

with $L(R_{11}) = L(R_{12}) = 2$ and $L(R_{13}) = 4$. Since $m > 3$ and $n > 3$, $d(G) = max\{m, n\} - 1 \geq 3$. So we have $L(R_{11}) = L(R_{12}) < L(R_{13}) \leq d(G) + 1$. For $w = 2$, $|F| = 1$, we can get $d(G - F; x_h y_g, x_p y_g) < d(G)$. For $w = 3$, $|F| = 2$. Even in the worst case, we can get $d(G - F; x_h y_g, x_p y_g) \leq d(G) + 1$.

Subsubcase 2. $1 < g < n$. There are three shortest paths R_7, R_{14} and R_{15} whose interior vertices are disjoint from $x_h y_g$ to $x_p y_g$ in G.

$$x_h y_g \rightarrow x_{h+1} y_{g+1} \rightarrow \cdots \rightarrow x_{p-1} y_{g+1} \rightarrow x_p y_g, \tag{14}$$

$$x_h y_g \rightarrow x_{h+1} y_{g-1} \rightarrow \cdots \rightarrow x_{p-1} y_{g-1} \rightarrow x_p y_g, \tag{15}$$

with $L(R_7) = L(R_{14}) = L(R_{15}) = p - h \leq m - 1 \leq max\{m, n\} - 1 = d(G)$. For $1 \leq w \leq 3$, $|F| = 2$, we have $d(G - F; x_h y_g, x_p y_g) \leq d(G)$.

Subcase 2. $x_h \neq x_p$ and $y_g \neq y_q$. According to whether the distances of any two vertices $x_h y_g$ and $x_p y_q$ on two factor graphs are equal, we can divide into the following two subcases.

Subsubcase 1. $p - h = q - g$. There are three internally vertex-disjoint paths R_{16}, R_{17} and R_{18} from $x_h y_g$ to $x_p y_q$ in G.

$$x_h y_g \rightarrow x_{h+1} y_{g+1} \rightarrow \cdots \rightarrow x_{p-1} y_{q-1} \rightarrow x_p y_q, \tag{16}$$

$$x_h y_g \rightarrow x_h y_{g+1} \rightarrow \cdots \rightarrow x_{p-1} y_q \rightarrow x_p y_q, \tag{17}$$

$$x_h y_g \rightarrow x_{h+1} y_g \rightarrow \cdots \rightarrow x_p y_{q-1} \rightarrow x_p y_q, \tag{18}$$

with $L(R_{16}) = p - h \leq m - 1 \leq max\{m, n\} - 1 = d(G)$ and $L(R_{17}) = L(R_{18}) = p - h + 1 \leq m \leq max\{m, n\} = d(G) + 1$. For $w = 2$, $|F| = 1$. Even in the worst case, we have $d(G - F; x_h y_g, x_p y_q) \leq d(G) + 1$. For $w = 3$, $|F| = 2$. Similarly, we can also get $d(G - F; x_h y_g, x_p y_q) \leq d(G) + 1$.

Subsubcase 2. $p - h \neq q - g$. Without loss of generality, we assume that $p - h > q - g$. Consider $q = n$, the vertex $x_p y_q$ has no neighbors above, we can only construct the internally vertex-disjoint paths which pass through the neighbors at the same level or below $x_p y_q$ in G. For $w = 2$, $|F| = 1$. There are two shortest paths R_{19} and R_{20} whose interior vertices are disjoint from $x_h y_g$ to $x_p y_q$ in G.

$$x_h y_g \rightarrow x_{h+1} y_g \rightarrow \cdots \rightarrow x_{p-q+g} y_g \rightarrow \cdots \rightarrow x_{p-1} y_{q-1} \rightarrow x_p y_q, \qquad (19)$$

$$x_h y_g \rightarrow x_{h+1} y_{g+1} \rightarrow \cdots \rightarrow x_{h+q-g} y_q \rightarrow \cdots \rightarrow x_{p-1} y_q \rightarrow x_p y_q, \qquad (20)$$

with $L(R_{19}) = L(R_{20}) = p - h \leq m - 1 \leq max\{m,n\} - 1 = d(G)$. Even in the worst case, we have $d(G - F; x_h y_g, x_p y_q) \leq d(G)$. For $w = 3$, $|F| = 2$. There are three internally vertex-disjoint paths R_{21}, R_{22} and R_{23} from $x_h y_g$ to $x_p y_q$ in G.

$$x_h y_g \rightarrow x_{h+1} y_{g+1} \rightarrow \cdots \rightarrow x_{h+q-g-1} y_{q-1} \rightarrow \cdots \rightarrow x_{p-1} y_{q-1} \rightarrow x_p y_q, \qquad (21)$$

$$x_h y_g \rightarrow x_h y_{g+1} \rightarrow \cdots \rightarrow x_{h+q-g-1} y_q \rightarrow \cdots \rightarrow x_{p-1} y_q \rightarrow x_p y_q, \qquad (22)$$

$$x_h y_g \rightarrow x_{h+1} y_g \rightarrow \cdots \rightarrow x_{p-q+g+1} y_g \rightarrow \cdots \rightarrow x_p y_{q-1} \rightarrow x_p y_q, \qquad (23)$$

with $L(R_{21}) = p - h \leq m - 1 \leq max\{m,n\} - 1 = d(G)$ and $L(R_{22}) = L(R_{23}) = p - h + 1 \leq m \leq max\{m,n\} = d(G) + 1$. Even in the worst case, we have $d(G - F; x_h y_g, x_p y_q) \leq d(G) + 1$.

Consider $g < q < n$, we construct the internally vertex-disjoint paths which can pass through the neighbors above $x_p y_q$. Different from the previous construction, we replace the neighbor $x_p y_{q-1}$ of $x_p y_q$ with $x_{p-1} y_{q+1}$. There are three internally vertex-disjoint paths R_{19}, R_{20} and R_{24} from $x_h y_g$ to $x_p y_q$ in G.

$$x_h y_g \rightarrow x_h y_{g+1} \rightarrow \cdots \rightarrow x_{h+q-g} y_{q+1} \rightarrow \cdots \rightarrow x_{p-1} y_{q+1} \rightarrow x_p y_q, \qquad (24)$$

with $L(R_{19}) = L(R_{20}) = p - h \leq m - 1 \leq max\{m,n\} - 1 = d(G)$ and $L(R_{24}) = p - h + 1 \leq m \leq max\{m,n\} = d(G) + 1$. For $w = 2$, $|F| = 1$. Even in the worst case, we have $d(G - F; x_h y_g, x_p y_q) \leq d(G)$. For $w = 3$, $|F| = 2$. In the worst case, we have $d(G - F; x_h y_g, x_p y_q) \leq d(G) + 1$.

In this case, we can conclude two results through analysis. If $m = n$, we can get $D_2(G) \leq d(G) + 1$ and $D_3(G) \leq d(G) + 1$. If $m \neq n$, we can get $D_2(G) \leq d(G)$ and $D_3(G) \leq d(G) + 1$. Consider their lower bounds, we give a specific set of faulty vertices. If $m = n$, let $F = \{x_{h+1} y_{g+1}\}$, we can get $D_2(G) \geq d(G) + 1$. Let $F = \{x_{h+1} y_{g+1}, x_h y_{g+1}\}$, we can get $D_3(G) \geq d(G) + 1$. Therefore, we have $D_2(G) = D_3(G) = d(G) + 1$. If $m \neq n$, let $F = \{x_{h+1} y_g, x_{h+1} y_{g+1}\}$, we can get $D_3(G) \geq d(G) + 1$. Therefore, we have $D_2(G) = d(G)$ and $D_3(G) = d(G) + 1$.

Case 4. $m = 3$, $n = 3$. For any $1 \leq w \leq 3$, we have $G - F$ is connected. The diameter of G is 2. For $w = 2$, $|F| = 1$, the result is the same as Case 3. For $w = 3$, $|F| = 2$. The construction method is the same as Case 3, we also can get that there are three internally vertex-disjoint paths of length at most 4 between any two vertices in G. So we have $D_3(G) \leq d(G) + 2$ in this case. Consider the lower bound, let $F = \{x_2 y_1, x_2 y_2\}$, we can get $d(G - F; x_1 y_1, x_3 y_1) = 4 = d(G) + 2$, such that $D_3(G) \geq d(G) + 2$. Therefore, we have $D_3(G) = d(G) + 2 = 4$. $\square$

The edge connectivity is the basic parameter necessary to discuss the edge fault diameter of interconnection networks, we give the edge connectivity of the strong product graph of two paths by the following lemma and corollary.

Lemma 5 ([3]). *Let G_1 and G_2 be two nontrivial connected graphs with orders $n_1, n_2 \geq 2$, edges c_1, c_2, the minimum degrees δ_1, δ_2 and the edge-connectivity λ_1, λ_2, respectively. Then*

$$\lambda(G_1 \boxtimes G_2) = min\{\lambda_1(n_2 + 2c_2), \lambda_2(n_1 + 2c_1), \delta_1 + \delta_2 + \delta_1\delta_2\}.$$

If G_1 and G_2 are two paths, we have $c_i = n_i - 1$ and $\delta_i = \lambda_i = 1$ for $i = 1, 2$, the following corollary can be directly determined.

Corollary 1. *Let P_m and P_n be two paths with orders $m, n \geq 2$, respectively. Then*

$$\lambda(P_m \boxtimes P_n) = 3.$$

Under the determined edge connectivity, we prove the following result by constructing edge-disjoint paths between any two vertices in strong product graph of two paths.

Theorem 2. *Let P_m and P_n be two paths with orders $m, n \geq 2$, respectively. Then for any $1 \leq t \leq 3$, we have*

$$D'_t(P_m \boxtimes P_n) = \begin{cases} max\{m,n\} - 1, & for\ t = 1, \\ max\{m,n\} - 1, & for\ t = 2\ and\ m \neq n, \\ max\{m,n\}, & for\ t = 2\cdot and\ m = n, \\ max\{m,n\}, & for\ t = 3. \end{cases}$$

Proof. Let $G = P_m \boxtimes P_n$ with $V(P_m) = \{x_1, \cdots, x_m\}$ and $V(P_n) = \{y_1, \cdots, y_n\}$, $x_h y_g$ and $x_p y_q$ are any two vertices in G, where $x_h, x_p \in V(P_m)$ and $y_g, y_q \in V(P_n)$. Let F be the faulty edge set of G with $|F| < t$.

By Corollary 1, we can get the edge connectivity of G is 3. By Lemma 4, we can get the diameter of G is $max\{m,n\} - 1$. For $w = 1$, there is no faulty edge in F, we have $D'_1(G) = d(G) = max\{m,n\} - 1$. We can discuss the following three cases.

Case 1. $m = 2$, $n = 2$. For any $1 \leq t \leq 3$, we have $G - F$ is connected. Since $P_2 \boxtimes P_2 = K_4$, we can get the diameter of G is 1 in this case. For a complete graph of order k, there are $k - 1$ edge-disjoint paths of length at most 2 between any two vertices. Among them, one edge connects the two vertices, and there are $k - 2$ paths of length 2 with the remaining $k - 2$ neighbors as intermediate vertices. Through this, we can get that there are three edge-disjoint paths between any two vertices in G. Among them, one path of length 1 and two paths of length 2. For $2 \leq t \leq 3$, $|F| = 2$. Even in the worst case, there is at least one path of length 2 connects the two vertices in $G - F$, we can get $D'_t(G) \leq 2 = d(G) + 1$. Consider the lower bound, if we remove the edge which connects the two vertices, we can get $D'_2(G) \geq 2 = d(G) + 1$. Therefore, we have $D'_t(G) = 2 = d(G) + 1$.

Case 2. $m \neq n$ or $m = n > 3$. It is easy to know that the internally vertex-disjoint paths are also edge-disjoint, and the reverse is not true.

If $m \neq n$, by Theorem 1, we can also get $D_2'(G) \leq d(G)$ and $D_3'(G) \leq d(G) + 1$. Let $F = \{(x_h y_g, x_{h+1} y_g), (x_h y_g, x_{h+1} y_{g+1})\}$, we can get $D_3'(G) \geq d(G) + 1$. Therefore, we have $D_2'(G) = d(G)$ and $D_3'(G) = d(G) + 1$.

If $m = n > 3$, by Theorem 1, we can also get $D_2'(G) \leq d(G) + 1$ and $D_3'(G) \leq d(G) + 1$. For $t = 2$, $|F| = 1$, let $F = \{(x_h y_g, x_{h+1} y_{g+1})\}$. If remove this edge, we can get the lower bound $D_2'(G) \geq d(G) + 1$. For $t = 3$, $|F| = 2$, let $F = \{(x_h y_g, x_{h+1} y_{g+1}), (x_h y_g, x_h y_{g+1})\}$. If remove the two edges, we can get the lower bound $D_3'(G) \geq d(G) + 1$. Therefore, we have $D_2'(G) = D_3'(G) = d(G) + 1$.

Case 3. $m = 3$, $n = 3$. For $t = 2$, $|F| = 1$, the result is the same as Case 2. For $w = 3$, $|F| = 2$. Consider the worst case of $y_g = y_q$ and $p - h = 2$. we construct three edge-disjoint paths R_{11}, R_{25} and R_{26} from $x_h y_g$ to $x_p y_g$ in G.

$$x_h y_g \rightarrow x_h y_{g+1} \rightarrow x_{h+1} y_{g+1} \rightarrow x_p y_g, \tag{25}$$

$$x_h y_g \rightarrow x_{h+1} y_{g+1} \rightarrow x_p y_{g+1} \rightarrow x_p y_g, \tag{26}$$

with $L(R_{11}) = 2$ and $L(R_{25}) = L(R_{26}) = 3$. Since the diameter of G is 2, we can get $L(R_{11}) < L(R_{25}) = L(R_{26}) = 3 = d(G) + 1$. For $2 \leq t \leq 3$, $|F| = 2$. Even in the worst case, we have $D_t'(G) \leq d(G) + 1$. By Case 2, the lower bound is $D_2'(G) \geq d(G) + 1$ and $D_3'(G) \geq d(G) + 1$. Therefore, we can also get $D_2'(G) = D_3'(G) = d(G) + 1$.   □

3   Model Comparison

The mesh network is a kind of static interconnection network, in which processors communicate directly through point-to-point connection [21]. It is widely used in system on chip, high-performance parallel and distributed systems [22]. The topology model of the mesh network is a Cartesian product graph of two paths, which is denoted by $G(m, n) = P_m \square P_n$. In [21], we can get the connectivity and edge connectivity of the mesh network are 2. The diameter of the mesh network is $m + n - 2$. For $w = 2$, $|F| = 1$. There are two internally vertex-disjoint paths of length at most $d(G)$ between any two vertices in the mesh network. Therefore, we have $D_2(G(m, n)) = D_2'(G(m, n)) = d(G) = m + n - 2$. The maximum diameters of the mesh network $G(4, 4)$ with one faulty vertex and one faulty edge are shown on Fig. 2.

Based on the mesh network, we give an improved mesh network. Its topology model is the strong product graph of two paths, which is denoted by $S(m, n) = P_m \boxtimes P_n$. In the previous results, we can get the connectivity of the improved mesh network is 2 or 3 and the edge connectivity of the improved mesh network is 3. The diameter of the improved mesh network is $max\{m, n\} - 1$. In order to compare the mesh network equally, we just consider the worst case of $m = n$ and $w = 2$. Therefore, we have $D_2(S(m, n)) = D_2'(S(m, n)) = d(G) + 1 = max\{m, n\}$. The maximum diameters of the improved mesh network $S(4, 4)$ with one faulty vertex and one faulty edge are shown on Fig. 3.

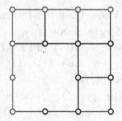
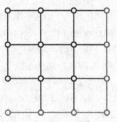

Fig. 2. The network $G(4,4)$ with one faulty vertex and one faulty edge.

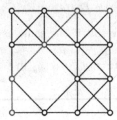
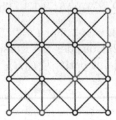

Fig. 3. The network $S(4,4)$ with one faulty vertex and one faulty edge.

According to Fig. 2 and Fig. 3, we can directly get that the two networks have the same number of vertices, but the improved mesh network has more edges than the mesh network. This means that the link cost is higher when building the improved mesh network than when building the mesh network. Since $\kappa(G(m,n)) \leq \kappa(S(m,n))$ and $\lambda(G(m,n)) < \lambda(S(m,n))$, the improved mesh network also has higher fault tolerance than the mesh network, which can allow more vertices or edges to fail and still ensure the normal operation of the network. From the previous results, we can get $d(S(m,n)) < d(G(m,n))$, the improved mesh network has a smaller transmission delay than the mesh network. This means that in the process of data transmission, the improved mesh network has higher effectiveness than the mesh network.

Compare the transmission delay of the two networks in the case of vertex failure, from the previous results, we can get $D_2(S(m,n)) \leq D_2(G(m,n))$. In this case, the transmission delay of the improved mesh network is smaller than that of the mesh network. This means that when the two networks have vertex failure, the improved mesh network still maintains a higher effectiveness than the mesh network. Compare the transmission delay of the two networks in the case of edge failure, we can also get $D_2'(S(m,n)) \leq D_2'(G(m,n))$. Similarly, this means that when the two networks have edge failure, the improved mesh network still maintains a higer effectiveness than the mesh network. We define the difference between the vertex fault diameters of the mesh network and the improved mesh network as $\Delta_1 = D_2(G(m,n)) - D_2(S(m,n))$, and the difference between the edge fault diameters of the mesh network and the improved mesh network as $\Delta_2 = D_2'(G(m,n)) - D_2'(S(m,n))$. Then we can get

$$\Delta_1 = \Delta_2 = m + n - 2 - max\{m, n\} = min\{m, n\} - 2.$$

Through formula, we can find that with the expansion of the two networks scale, the two differences are also increasing, the advantage of information transmission effectiveness of the improved mesh network is more obvious than that of the mesh network.

Compared with the mesh network, the improved mesh network also has its own application characteristics. In the topology model of the improved mesh network, all edges are required to be independent of each other, there is no case that one edge fails and affects the information transmission of other edges. Therefore, the edge intersection is not allowed in the hardware design of the improved mesh network. Moreover, we can also find that there are two kinds of edges in the topology model of the improved mesh network. If the two endpoints of an edge have a pair of equal coordinates and a pair of coordinates whose values differ by 1, it is called a common edge. If the two endpoints of an edge have two pairs of coordinates whose values differ by 1, it is called a bevel edge. Obviously, the bevel edge is longer than the common edge. From this, the construction cost of bevel edge is higher, if it wants to keep the synchronization of sending and receiving information between adjacent vertices in a longer transmission distance than the common edge. In order to better handle edges with different costs, we define an edge as a unit, let the unit cost of common edge be a_1 and the unit cost of bevel edge be a_2, where $a_1 < a_2$. In the topology model of the improved mesh network, the number of common edges is $m(n - 1) + n(m - 1)$ and the number of bevel edges is $2(m - 1)(n - 1)$. When building a large-scale improved mesh network $S(m, n)$, the link cost function C_l is

$$C_l = (2mn - m - n)a_1 + 2(m - 1)(n - 1)a_2.$$

Through the link cost function C_l, for an improved mesh network of a given size, no matter how large, the link cost is easy to obtain. However, there are still some limitations on the application of the improved mesh network. The improved mesh network requires that the processor can process data in up to 8 links at the same time. Compared with the parallel processing ability of data in up to 4 links of the mesh network, the improved mesh network requires higher processor performance, this also increases processor cost. For the number of edges ϵ, there is also an upper limit.

$$\epsilon \leq 4mn - 3m - 3n + 2.$$

In this range of the number of edges, the advantages of the improved mesh network can be fully exerted.

When the size of the topology model of the improved mesh network is very large, the corresponding link cost is very high. However, with the expansion of the scale, the improved mesh network will have greater advantages in normal transmission efficiency, fault transmission efficiency, fault tolerance and reliability. So even for large-scale structures, the topology model of the improved mesh network is also applicable, especially for large-scale parallel computer systems.

4   Conclusions

With the development of supercomputers and parallel computing systems, high
requirements are put forward for the fault tolerance capability and the information transmission capability under fault of network models. In this paper, the
vertex fault diameter and edge fault diameter of strong product graph of two
paths are given. Through the results, we find that the strong product graph of
two paths have small vertex fault diameter and small edge fault diameter. Then
we propose an improved mesh network, whose model is the strong product graph
of two paths and has high fault tolerance and high effectiveness, this provides a
new method for designing the topological structure of large-scale interconnection
networks.

References

1. Sabidussi, G.: Graph multiplication. Math. Z. **72**(1), 446–457 (1959)
2. Sun, L., Xu, J.M.: Connectivity of strong product graphs. J. Univ. Sci. Technol. China **36**(3), 236–241 (2006)
3. Yang, C., Xu, J.M.: Connectivity and edge-connectivity of strong product graphs. J. Univ. Sci. Technol. China **5**(5), 449–455 (2008)
4. Špacapan, S.: Connectivity of strong products of graphs. Graph. Combinator. **26**(3), 457–467 (2010)
5. Liang, D., Li, F., Xu, Z.B.: The number of spanning trees in a new lexicographic product of graphs. Sci. China Inf. Sci. **57**(11), 1–9 (2014). https://doi.org/10.1007/s11432-014-5110-z
6. Li, F., Wang, W., Xu, Z.B., Zhao, H.X.: Some results on the lexicographic product of vertex-transitive graphs. Appl. Math. Lett. **24**(11), 1924–1926 (2011)
7. Geetha, J., Somasundaram, K.: Total colorings of product graphs. Graph. Combinator. **34**(2), 339–347 (2018)
8. Chung, F.R.K., Garey, M.R.: Diameter bounds for altered graphs. J. Graph Theory **8**(4), 511–534 (1984)
9. Dankelmann, P.: Bounds on the fault-diameter of graphs. Networks **70**(2), 132–140 (2017)
10. Du, D.Z., Hsu, D.F., Lyuu, Y.D.: On the diameter vulnerability of Kautz digraphs. Discrete Math. **151**(1–3), 81–85 (1996)
11. Esfahanian, A.H., Hakimi, S.L.: Fault-tolerant routing in Debruijn communication networks. IEEE Trans. Comput. **34**(9), 777–788 (1985)
12. Cao, F., Du, D.Z., Hsu, F., Teng, S.H.: Fault tolerance properties of pyramid networks. IEEE Trans. Comput. **46**(1), 88–93 (1999)
13. Latifi, S.: On the fault-diameter of the star graph. Inform. Process. Lett. **46**(3), 143–150 (1993)
14. Chen, X.B.: Edge-fault-tolerant diameter and bipanconnectivity of hypercubes. Inform. Process. Lett. **110**(24), 1088–1092 (2010)
15. Ma, M., West, D.B., Xu, J.M.: The vulnerability of the diameter of the enhanced hypercubes. Theor. Comput. Sci. **694**, 60–65 (2017)
16. Qi, H., Zhu, X.: The fault-diameter and wide-diameter of twisted hypercubes. Discrete Appl. Math. **235**, 154–160 (2018)

17. Xu, M., Xu, J.M., Hou, X.M.: Fault diameter of Cartesian product graphs. Inform. Process. Lett. **93**(5), 245–248 (2005)
18. Banič, I., Žerovnik, J.: The fault-diameter of Cartesian products. Adv. Appl. Math. **40**(1), 98–106 (2008)
19. Banič, I., Erveš, R., Žerovnik, J.: The edge fault-diameter of Cartesian graph bundles. Eur. J. Combin. **30**(5), 1054–1061 (2009)
20. Hammack, R., Imrich, W., Klavžar, S.: Handbook of Product Graphs, 2nd edn. CRC Press, Boca Raton (2011)
21. Leighton, F.T.: Introduction to Parallel Algorithms and Architectures: Arrays, Trees, Hypercubes, 1st edn. Morgan Kaufmann Publishers, San Mateo (1992)
22. Rajkumar, S., Goyal, N.K.: Reliable multistage interconnection network design. Peer-to-Peer Netw. Appl. **9**(6), 979–990 (2016)

Design and Implementation of SF Selection Based on Distance and SNR Using Autonomous Distributed Reinforcement Learning in LoRa Networks

Ikumi Urabe[1]([⊠]), Aohan Li[2], Minoru Fujisawa[1], Song-Ju Kim[1,3],
and Mikio Hasegawa[1]

[1] Tokyo University of Science, Shinjuku City, Tokyo 125-8585, Japan
`4321510@ed.tus.ac.jp`
[2] The University of Electro-Communications, Chofu, Tokyo 182-8585, Japan
[3] SOBIN Institute LLC, Kawanishi, Hyogo 666-0145, Japan

Abstract. LoRaWAN, one of Low-Power-Wide-Area (LPWA), has been deployed in many IoT applications due to its ability to communicate over long distances and low power consumption. However, the scalability and communication performance of LoRaWAN is highly dependent on Spreading Factor (SF) and Channel (CH) allocation. In particular, it is important to configure SF appropriately according to the distance of the LoRa device from the GateWay (GW) and the environment. In this paper, we implement and evaluate lightweight distributed reinforcement learning-based SF selection methods. This method allows each IoT device to make appropriate parameter selections without requiring any prior information, but only utilizing ACKnowledge obtained from its own transmissions. We then conducted real experiments in a small area indoors to verify that each LoRa device can autonomously and decentralized perform appropriate SF selection in response to the distance from the GW and SNR that varies depending on the surrounding environment. The results show that the implemented methods can select appropriate SF and achieve a better Frame Success Rate (FSR) than other lightweight approaches.

Keywords: IoT · LoRaWAN · Lightweight Distributed Reinforcement Learning · SF Selection

1 Introduction

IoT communication requires high energy efficiency, long-distance communication, and low cost, and a communication method called Low-Power-Wide-Area (LPWA), which satisfies these requirements, is attracting attention. LoRa, Sigfox, LTE-Cat, and NB-IoT are well-known LPWA networks. Among them, LoRaWAN has been adopted in many IoT applications because it is a low-cost and open-standard communication method.

Y. Kambayashi et al. (Eds.): AICON 2022, LNICST 477, pp. 34–42, 2023.
https://doi.org/10.1007/978-3-031-29126-5_3

With the rapid growth of LoRa devices, improving the scalability of LoRaWAN has become a major challenge.

LoRa networks use chirped spread spectrum (CSS) modulation. CSS is a spread spectrum technique that uses a chirp signal whose frequency increases linearly with time, making LoRaWAN highly resistant to interference. And its Spreading Factor (SF) determines the bit rate and reception sensitivity, which are in a trade-off relationship. In other words, The smaller the SF, the higher the transmission speed and the shorter the transmission time, but a high Signal to Noise Ratio (SNR) is required. Therefore, packets cannot be received by the GW unless the SF is appropriate for each LoRa device's distance from the GW and the surrounding conditions. From these, SF allocation has a significant impact on communication performance in LoRaWAN and must be optimized for each IoT application. Besides the access SF, the Channel (CH) is another important factor affecting the communication performance of LoRaWAN. And since packet collisions occur only when two or more devices choose the same CH and SF, the scalability of LoRaWAN is highly dependent on those parameter assignments.

Most of the research on parameter selection methods in LoRaWAN is based on a scheme called the centralized approach. In this approach, the GW assigns transmission parameters to each device. However, in the centralized approach, the GW needs to know all the information in advance, such as the number of devices, the location of each device, and the probability of an event occurring. Furthermore, each IoT device is required to be in a waking state to receive control signals from the GW, which increases battery consumption, and the occupancy of the channel by control signals increases transmission resource consumption. It also fails to account for interference from IoT devices in other applications that the GW is not aware of or from electronic devices emitting leaky radio waves, which has serious implications in the current environment of rapidly growing IoT devices. On the other hand, the distributed approach allows each device to make autonomous choices without requiring prior information, and the use of lightweight reinforcement learning algorithms allows for low-cost parameter optimization in terms of power and memory consumption.

In this paper, we implement and evaluate the Multi-Armed-Bandit (MAB) based decentralized SF selection methods. Each device is considered an intelligent agent, which is rewarded with Acknowledgement (ACK) information and chooses transmission parameters to maximize the cumulative reward. In [5], a channel selection method using the MAB algorithm was proposed, but it takes a huge number of iteration for the parameter selection of each device to converge, which is impractical in real environments where communication congestion is constantly and dynamically changing. In [6, 7], an algorithm called Tug-of-War (ToW) -dynamics was proposed, which is a small amount of calculation and a highly efficient search method for dynamically changing environments. Also in [8–10], ToW-dynamics is applied to the channel selection problem in wireless networks, and the proposed approach is implemented in IoT devices to verify its effectiveness. In this paper, we focus on SF selection in LoRa, implement the proposed method based ToW-dynamics [8] in a real LoRa device, and conduct experiments in a small indoor area. The goal of ToW-dynamics is to improve scalability by allowing each LoRa device to autonomously and decentrally select the SF with the least collisions and based on distance and surrounding environment. To demonstrate the performance of the proposed approach, we evaluate the Frame Success Rates (FSR) and compare them with other lightweight techniques using our LoRa devices equipped with the SF selection algorithms, which are located in an experimental field with different distances.

2 System Model and Problem Formulation

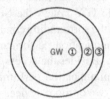

Fig. 1. System Model.

In this paper, we consider the star topology of LoRaWAN and assume a network with one GW and L LoRa devices. D is the LoRa device set, where D_l denotes the lth LoRa device. The LoRa devices are located in several locations, each at a different distance from the GW (Fig. 1). Assuming that the number of SFs is S, each LoRa device selects one SF among them to transmit packets. As shown in Sect. 1, LoRa employs chirp spread spectrum modulation so that signals with different SF (7–12) can be identified and received even if they are transmitted simultaneously on the same channel. And different SFs have different transmission speeds and different thresholds for the SNR that can be received. Table 1 shows the relationship between the bit rate and reception threshold. Theoretically, each spreading code is orthogonal, so collisions occur when two or more LoRa devices choose the same SF and CH. In practice, however, perfect orthogonality is not guaranteed, and interference between transmission using different SFs on the same CH must be considered [11, 12].

Each device selects not only the SF, but also the bandwidth from 62.5, 125, 250, and 500 [kHz], the transmit power from −4–13 [dBm], and the channel from 1–15 [CH]. In this paper, for ease of performance evaluation, we assume that all devices set the bandwidth to 125 kHz, the transmit power to maximum, and use the same channel. We also assume that all devices transmit M-byte packets of the same length with the same transmission interval TI.

A lightweight distributed reinforcement learning approach is implemented in each LoRa device and learns using ACK. At each decision, the device is considered as an intelligent agent that needs to strategically select SF based on the reinforcement learning approach. After decision and transmission, the LoRa device waits for ACK from the GW. If the transmission is successful, the LoRa device receives the ACK; otherwise, it does not. It is also assumed that there is no collision between this ACK and the uplink transmission. If ACK is not received, the packet is considered lost due to a collision with another packet transmitted on the same SF, or due to inter-SF interference.

In this paper, FSR was used to evaluate each approach. FSR in the LoRaWAN system at the t-th decision is defined as the ratio of the number of successful transmissions to

Table 1. LoRa Modulation Parameters at BW = 125 kHz.

SF	Bit Rate [kbps]	Receiver Sensitility [dBm]	SNR Thresh [dB]	Inter-SF collision Thresh [dB]
7	5.47	−123	−6	−7.5
8	3.13	−126	−9	−9
9	1.76	−129	−12	−13.5
10	0.98	−132	−15	−15
11	0.54	−133	−17.5	−18
12	0.29	−136	−20	−22.5

the total number of transmission attempts at the t-th decision and is expressed as:

$$FSR(t) = \sum_{m=1}^{M} \frac{r_t(t)}{n_l(t)} \tag{1}$$

where n_l is the number of transmission attempts at device l and r_l is the number of successful transmissions, i.e., the number of ACKs received. The objective function is expressed by the following equation:

$$(P) \quad \max \sum_{t=1}^{T} FSR(t) \tag{2}$$

3   SF Parameter Selection for ToW-Dynamics

3.1   Multi-armed Bandit Problem

In the Multi-Armed Bandit (MAB) problem, a player selects a slot machine to play from among several slot machines. The player aims to maximize the amount of coins he or she earns by playing repeatedly. The player does not know the coin payout probability of each slot machine but finds the slot machine that gives the most coins by repeated play. In order to find a good slot machine that pays more coins, the player must search by playing various slot machines, i.e., by playing slot machines other than the one that currently has the best probability of paying out more coins. On the other hand, if we search more than necessary, we will not be able to increase the number of coins, so if we can estimate a good slot machine, we must increase the number of coins by playing that slot machine.

As shown in Sect. 2 our goal is to maximize the cumulative FSR by having each device autonomously select the appropriate SF using only the local information available to it (received ACKs), and this learning can be addressed in the MAB framework: an IoT device (player) has S SFs (slot machines), and the objective is to maximize the cumulative FSR (cumulative rewards).

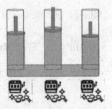

Fig. 2. ToW-dynamics.

3.2 ToW-Dynamics Based SF Selection

In this paper, we implement an approach for solving two MAB problems with SF selection using ToW-dynamics [6–8]. ToW-dynamics has been analytically validated for its high efficiency, despite its simplicity and low computational complexity, in making a series of decisions to maximize the probabilistic reward obtained, even in dynamic environments where reward probabilities frequently change [6–8]. The essential element of ToW-dynamics is a volume-conserving physical object, assuming, for example, that each slot machine is assigned to multiple cylinders with branches containing incompressible fluid, as shown in Fig. 2. The volume is updated by pushing and pulling the corresponding cylinder depending on whether or not the slot machine is rewarded for a trial at time t. Since the cylinders are connected, as in Fig. 2, the volume increase in one part immediately compensates for volume decreases in others. In other words, ToW-dynamics can update reward estimates for slot machines that are not actually played, which is the reason for its high performance. In ToW-dynamics, the arm k^* with the height cylinder interface value X is selected, and X_k is expressed by the following formula:

$$X_k(t) = Q_k(t-1) - \frac{1}{U - 1_{k' \neq k}} \sum Q_{k'}(t-1) + osc_k(t) \qquad (3)$$

$$osc_k(t) = A cos\left(\frac{2\pi(t+k-1)}{U}\right) \qquad (4)$$

The osc_k is a fluctuation term, and the inclusion of this fluctuation allows the algorithm to perform properly for exploration and exploitation. U is the number of arms, which in SF selection is the number of available SFs $S.Q_k$ is the reward estimate of the kth arm and is derived by the following equation:

$$Q_k(t) = \begin{cases} \alpha Q_k(t-1) + \Delta Q_k(t), & \text{if } k = k^* \\ \alpha Q_k(t-1) & \text{otherwise.} \end{cases} \qquad (5)$$

where α $(0 < \alpha \leq 1)$ is the decay parameter for reward estimation. ΔQ_k is given by the following Eq. (6).

$$\Delta Q_k(t) = \begin{cases} +1 & \text{if receiving ACK} \\ -\omega_j & \text{if not receiving ACK} \end{cases} \qquad (6)$$

In other words, if the transmission is successful and ACK is received, the Q value of the selected arm's (parameter's) gains " $+1$" as a reward, increasing the height of the fluid interface. Conversely, when the transmission fails and ACK is not received, the corresponding arm (parameter) is updated with the punishment $-\omega$, decreasing the interface value of the arm and increasing the interface value of the other arm. Here $-\omega$ is expressed:

$$\omega(t) = \frac{p_{1st}(t) + p_{2nd}(t)}{2 - p_{1st}(t) - p\quad(t)} \tag{7}$$

where p_{1st} and p_{2nd} are the highest and second highest reward probabilities in the arm at time t, respectively. The reward probability p is given by the following equation:

$$p(t) = \frac{R_k(t)}{N_k(t)} \tag{8}$$

where N_k is the number of times arm k was selected by time t, and R_k is the number of successful transmissions. N_k and R_k are derived by:

$$N_k(t) = \begin{cases} 1 + \beta N_k(t-1) & \text{if } k = k \\ \beta N_k(t-1) & \text{otherwise} \end{cases} \tag{9}$$

$$R_k(t) = \begin{cases} 1 + \beta R_k(t-1) & \text{if } k = k^* \text{ and receiving ACK} \\ \beta R_k(t-1) & \text{otherwise} \end{cases} \tag{10}$$

where β $(0 < \beta \le 1)$ is the forgetting rate for learning and success experience.

In this method, each device does not need to keep information about packets it has sent in the past and only needs to keep the values of Q_k, N_k and R_k, hence memory consumption is only $S \times \{size\ of\ bits\ (Q_k, + N_k + R_k)\}$ is all that is needed. Also, since each device only needs to decide which SF to use in each iteration, the computational complexity is $O(1)$.

4   Implementation and Performance Evaluation

The proposed method is implemented in a wireless module that supports LoRaWAN communication in the 920 MHz band. A Raspberry Pi was used for the GW and a battery-powered Arduino mini pro was used for the LoRa device. And each device is equipped with an ES 920LR module that supports LoRaWAN communication (Fig. 3). The implemented LoRaWAN system is used to evaluate the performance of the ToW-dynamics-based transmit parameter selection approach compared to i) UCB1-based, ii) ε-greedy based, iii) random-based transmit parameter selection. The experiments were conducted indoors and LoRa devices were placed in several rooms (Fig. 4). The LoRa device in position 1 was installed in the same room as the GW, guaranteeing a LOS path, while the devices in positions 2 and 3 were installed in another room at a distance from the GW, resulting in an NLOS path, and the Received Signal Strength Indication (RSSI) from each location is shown in Table 2. Therefore, devices at those distances from the GW should select a higher SF due to the lower received strength at the GW. To evaluate the impact of parameter selection in the network, we considered two scenarios, one with only SF selection and the other with SF-CH selection, using the proposed approach.

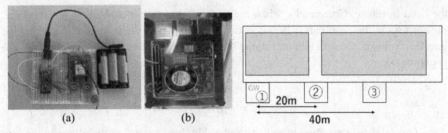

Fig. 3. (a) LoRa Device. (b) GateWay   Fig. 4. Experimental Field

Table 2. RSSI from each location.

Location	RSSI [dBm]
1	−57
2	−106
3	−116

In this scenario, the performance of SF selection is evaluated when all LoRa devices use a single channel. In this experiment, the transmission interval was set as 30 s. The forgetting rate α and β in ToW-dynamics were set to 0.9, and the parameter ε, which determines the search rate in ε-greedy, was set to 0.1. Other parameters used in the experiments are summarized in Table 3.

Table 3. Parameters for performance analysis in SF selection.

Parameter	Value
BandWidth	125 kHz
Number of devices L	3,9,15,30
SF	7, 8, 9
Transmission Interval I	20
Payload Length M	50 bytes
Transmission power P	13 dBm

Figure 5 summarizes the FSR for each selected approach when the number of LoRa devices is varied from 3 to 30 (3, 9, 15, 30). The number of devices at each location is equal, i.e., one device at each location for 3 devices and 10 devices at each location for 30 devices. From Fig. 5, it can be seen that the FSR decreases as the number of LoRa devices increases for all approaches. This is due to the increase in packet collisions as the number of LoRa devices increases. In addition, the method using the MAB algorithm has a higher FSR, indicating that the autonomous distributed reinforcement learning approach is effective. Among them, the proposed method obtains higher FSR than other methods using reinforcement learning, which makes it suitable for LoRaWAN systems. Figure 6 shows the ratio of SF selection per deployment location when there are 30 LoRa devices using ToW-dynamics approach. Packets from LoRa devices located at positions 2 and 3, which are far away from the GW, have weak reception strength at the GW, so a high SF should be selected. In other words, the proposed method does not require prior information on the distance to the GW, and the SF selection is appropriate for each LoRa device.

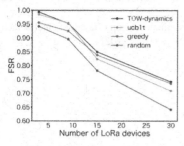

Fig. 5. FSR for SF selection

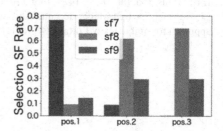

Fig. 6. SF selection at each location (TOW-dynamics)

5 Conclusion

In this paper, we propose a lightweight distributed reinforcement learning-based parameter selection method to address the LoRa network congestion problem. The approach can be implemented for LoRa devices with limited memory and computing power, and was evaluated in real-world experiments. Experimental results show that the proposed method can achieve higher FSR than other lightweight approaches. For future perspectives, there remains a need to select other parameters such as transmit power and bandwidth.

References

1. Shen, L.-H., et al.: Analysis and implementation for traffic-aware channel assignment and contention scheme in LoRa-based IoT networks. IEEE Internet Things J. **8**(14), 11368–11383 (2021)
2. Saluja, D., et al.: Scalability analysis of LoRa network for SNR-based SF allocation scheme. IEEE Trans. Ind. Inf. **17**(10), 6709–6719 (2021)
3. Lim, J.-T., et al.: Spreading factor allocation for massive connectivity in LoRa systems. IEEE Commun. Lett. **22**(4), 800–803 (2018)
4. Hamdi, R., et al.: Dynamic spreading factor assignment in LoRa wireless networks. In: ICC, pp. 1–5 (2020)
5. Ta, D.-T., et al.: LoRa-MAB: toward an intelligent resource allocation approach for LoRaWAN. In: GLOBECOM, pp. 1–6 (2019)
6. Kim, S.-J., et al.: Tug-of-war model for the two-bandit problem: nonlocally-correlated parallel exploration via resource conservation. BioSystems **101**, 29–36 (2010)

7. Kim, S.-J., et al.: Efficient decision-making by volume-conserving physical object. New J. Phys. **17**, 083023 (2015)
8. Ma, J., et al.: A reinforcement-learning-based distributed resource selection algorithm for massive IoT. Appl. Sci. **9**(18), 3730–3745 (2019)
9. Yamamoto, D., et al.: Performance evaluation of reinforcement learning based distributed channel selection algorithm in massive IoT networks. IEEE Access. **10**, 67870–67882 (2022)
10. Hasegawa, S., et al.: Multi-armed-bandit based channel selection algorithm for massive heterogeneous internet of things networks. Appl. Sci. **12**(15), 7424–7443 (2022)
11. Mahmood, A., et al.: Scalability analysis of a LoRa network under imperfect orthogonality. IEEE Trans. Ind. Inf. **15**(3), 1425–1436 (2019)
12. Li, A., et al.: A lightweight decentralized reinforcement learning based channel selection approach for high-density LoRaWAN. In: DySPAN, pp. 9–14 (2021)

Machine Learning

QBRT: Bias and Rising Threshold Algorithm with Q-Learning
Implementation of the Tower of Hanoi

Ryo Ogino[✉], Masao Kubo, and Hiroshi Sato

National Defense Academy, 1-10-20, Hashirimizu, Yokosuka, Kanagawa, Japan
em60010@nda.ac.jp

Abstract. In multi-agent reinforcement learning, the problems of non-stationarity of the environment and scalability have long been recognized. As a first step toward solving these problems, this paper proposes a learning model, the BRT Algorithm with Q-Learning (hereafter, QBRT), based on the Bias and Rising Threshold (hereafter, BRT) algorithm, which can solve best-of-n problems where the number of options n is greater than 2 (hereafter, best-of-n problems ($n >> 2$)). This model is characterized by the fact that all of the agents that make up the herd agree in advance on what action the herd will take next. We thought that the problem of non-stationarity could be ameliorated to some extent by having all agents follow the same policy. On the other hand, the time it takes for agents to reach an agreement with each other generally tends to increase as the number of agents increases. In contrast, if BRT is used as a base, the time required for agreement could be kept almost constant even if the number of agents increases. We will validate the problem with an experiment using Tower of Hanoi by Multiagent (hereafter THM), a best-of-n problem ($n >> 2$) based on the classic puzzle "Tower of Hanoi", which is a flock coordination problem.

Keywords: Multi-agent · Reinforcement learning · Best-of-n problem · Tower of Hanoi

1 Introduction

Among machine learning, reinforcement learning is being applied and studied for various tasks because of its ability to maximize earned rewards in the future. Here, the subject of reinforcement learning is called the agent. There are multi-agent systems in which multiple agents interact in the same environment and learn how to solve a task simultaneously. In recent years, there have been many attempts to extend single-agent reinforcement learning algorithms for multiple agents [1]. However, direct implementation of single-agent reinforcement learning algorithms on multiple agents is known to cause problems such as environment non-stationarity and scalability [1]. Non-stationarity is the problem that even if one agent takes certain all agents is the joint action, it will not converge to the optimal solution because different rewards are given depending on the

Y. Kambayashi et al. (Eds.): AICON 2022, LNICST 477, pp. 45–59, 2023.
https://doi.org/10.1007/978-3-031-29126-5_4

actions taken by other agents and the environment is not stationary [2]. Therefore, previous studies have proposed solutions to non-stationarity, such as a method that combines the Q tables of all agents [3] and a method that differentiates between the rate of increase and decrease of Q values [4]. However, these studies have only been implemented with a small number of agents (2–4) and have not been validated with a larger number of agents. On the other hand, the scalability problem is the problem that the size of the action space increases exponentially with the number of agents when the action space of all agents is in the joint action space of all agents [5]. Therefore, scalability solutions have been proposed, including those based on local observations [6] and those based on deep reinforcement learning [7]. Wang et al.. Also point out that there is a trade-off between the non-stationarity problem and the scalability problem [2], and an algorithm that can solve both of these problems is needed.

Here, we introduce the Bias and Rising Threshold (hereafter, BRT) algorithm [8] to the agent as a solution to the problems of non-stationarity and scalability. The BRT algorithm was proposed by Phung et al.. to enable a swarm of robots to handle a large number of options ($n >> 2$) in a best-of-n problem. Experiments have shown that this algorithm is able to select an alternative that is generally constant in time without being significantly affected by the number of agents in the herd. On the other hand, the BRT algorithm does not have a mechanism to take advantage of past experience and is an approximately random search, which can be inefficient in some cases. Therefore, we propose a multi-agent learning model that combines reinforcement learning and the BRT algorithm, in which all the constituent agents agree in advance on what action the herd will take next. We thought that the problem of non-stationarity could be ameliorated to some extent by having all agents follow the same policy. On the other hand, the time it takes for agents to reach an agreement with each other generally tends to increase as the number of agents increases. In contrast, if BRT is used as a base, the time required for agreement could be kept almost constant even if the number of agents increases. As a first step, we propose a learning BRT algorithm, BRT Algorithm with Q-Learning (hereafter QBRT), which can solve best-of-n problems (hereafter best-of-n problems ($n >> 2$)) where the number of options n is greater than 2.

Here, as a best-of-n problem ($n >> 2$), we experimented with Tower of Hanoi by Multiagent; THM, based on the classic puzzle Tower of Hanoi. If a conventional herd of BRT agents with random behavior is applied to THM as it is, it is not easy to solve the puzzle because the state of the tower changes each time due to the herd's behavior. On the other hand, when the learning BRT algorithm is applied to THM, the learning results in solving the puzzle much faster than the traditional BRT algorithm. QBRT, an application of the BRT algorithm, was able to achieve a herd that could promptly choose an appropriate option from a large number of options depending on the environment, even for a herd with a large number of agents. QBRT can be a stepping stone to reinforcement learning models that can address non-stationarity and scalability issues. In the future, we hope to see applications that handle more options with a larger number of agents, such as automated delivery and search and rescue at disaster sites.

Subsequent parts of this section are organized as follows. In Sect. 2, a brief intro-
duction to related research is given. In Sect. 3, a learning BRT algorithm is proposed, In
Sect. 4, the effectiveness of the proposed method is verified by computer experiments.
Finally, in Sect. 5, we present our conclusions.

2   Related Studies

We propose a learning BRT algorithm, QBRT, which can solve the best-of-n problem
(n >> 2). As a related study, this chapter begins with a brief introduction to previous
research on environment non-stationarity and scalability issues in Sect. 2.1. The BRT
algorithm is described next in Sect. 2.2. Section 2.3 describes the best-of-n problem
addressed in this study. Finally, we describe Q-learning, which was used for the learning
rules of the learning BRT algorithm in Sect. 2.4.

2.1   Prior Work on Environment Non-stationarity and Scalability Issues

According to a review by Canese et al. [1], the issues that must be considered when
extending from single-agent reinforcement learning algorithms to multi-agent scenarios
are the non-stationarity of the environment and scalability issues. Non-stationarity of the
environment is the problem that even if one agent takes certain same action, it will not
converge to the optimal solution because different rewards are given by the actions taken
by other agents and the environment will not be stationary [2]. On the other hand, the
scalability problem is the problem that the size of the action space increases exponentially
with the number of agents when the action space of all agents is in the joint action space
of all agents [5]. The following is a brief review of previous studies on these issues.

Studies on non-stationarity include those by Matta et al. [3] and Matignon et al. [4].
Matta et al. used a "centralized aggregation center" to combine the Q-value tables of
all agents and create a global Q-value table containing the highest and lowest Q-values,
representing the most highly rated iterations [3]. Matignon et al. propose an optimistic
agent that makes the rate of decrease in Q values smaller than the rate of increase when
Q values decrease due to learning [4]. This reduces the possibility of being punished for
the bad behavior of other agents, even if they have made the best options. On the other
hand, these studies have only been implemented with a small number of agents (2–4)
and have not been validated with a larger number of agents.

As a study of scalability issues, Kar et al. proposed QD-learning, a distributed version of Q-learning, in which the size of the action space is limited under the assumption
that each agent knows only its local actions and rewards and that the inter-agent communication network is weakly connected QD-learning, a distributed version of Q-learning,
has been proposed [6]. On the other hand, a method to approximate Q values using deep
reinforcement learning (DRL) has also been proposed [7].

2.2 BRT Algorithm

The Bias and Rising Threshold (hereafter, BRT) algorithm [8] is a herd decision-making framework that can handle a large number of options ($M \geq 2$) in a best-of-n problem. A swarm $A = \{A_i : i = 1, ..., N\}$ consisting of N agents is given an action set $O = \{o_j : j = 1, ..., M\}(M \geq 2)$. If agent A_i satisfies Eq. (1), the option $O_i(t + 1)$ to be selected at the next time continues to be the currently selected option $O_i(t)$; otherwise, $O_i(t + 1)$ is stochastically changed to an option other than $O_i(t)$.

$$\frac{n(O_i(t))}{N} \geq \theta_i + \tau \cdot c_i(t) \cdot (t - t_{i,last}(t)) \tag{1}$$

where $n(O_i(t))/N$ is the percentage of agents in the entire population who choose the same option as themselves, θ_i is the bias value of the individual attribute ($0 < \theta_i < 1$), and τ is a constant corresponding to the assumed value of the increase in supporters. $t_{i,last}(t)$ is the time when agent A_i last changed its option, and $(t - t_{i,last}(t))$ is the time it continues to choose the same option, represented by Eq. (2).

$$t_{i,last}(t) = \begin{cases} t & O_i(t) \neq O_i(t-1) \\ t_{i,last}(t-1) & otherwise \end{cases} \tag{2}$$

$c(t)$ is an evaluation function that is zero when the option expressed in Eq. (3) is feasible.

$$c_i(t) = c(t) = \begin{cases} 0 & \forall i, O_i \equiv o_{goal} \\ 1 & otherwise \end{cases} \tag{3}$$

o_{goal} is a suitable option $\left(o_{goal} \in O\right)$ to look for. Each agent does not know the o_{goal} in advance and decides to continue or change its option, taking into account the overall trend of the swarm. The state in which all agents select the same option is called the consensus state; otherwise, it is called the non-consensus state. Various behaviors can occur depending on the distribution of this individual attribute θ_i. Phung et al. report that using the distribution in Eq. (4), if the agreed-upon option is not o_{goal}, then over time, Eq. (1) is no longer satisfied and the state of agreement is broken, instantly causing the herd to agree again on a different option, and this creates behavior that repeats until agreement on o_{goal} is reached.

$$n(\theta_i) = \begin{cases} 0 & \theta_i \leq 0 \\ k_1 N \theta_i^2 & 0 < \theta_i < \frac{1}{M} \\ k_1 N \left(\theta_i - \frac{2}{M}\right)^2 & \frac{1}{M} < \theta_i < \frac{2}{M} \\ 0 & \frac{2}{M} \leq \theta_i \end{cases} \tag{4}$$

where $k_1 = (3M^3)/2$ is the normalization term.

This algorithm can be used in swarms with a large number of agents or with variable numbers of agents since experiments have shown that the number of agents, N, has little effect on the time required for consensus building. Because the BRT algorithm has the property that the swarm can agree on a single option even as the number of agents increases, a learning algorithm based on the BRT algorithm can be an algorithm that addresses the problem of non-stationarity and scalability in the environment.

2.3 Best-of-n Problem

The best-of-n problem is one of the problems related to swarm decision making. The problem is that the swarm chooses the best option to meet the current needs of the swarm from the n options available to it. There are still few studies dealing with the best-of-n problem with n >> 2 according to Valentini et al. [9]. Here we treat THM as a best-of-n problem with n >> 2 best-of-n problem, which is an application of the classical puzzle Tower of Hanoi on the theme of swarm coordination problems.

2.4 Q Learning

Q learning [8] is a type of reinforcement learning technique in which the Q value, the future value of a state/action pair, is empirically acquired through trial and error. The Q value is the total amount of reward that a given action in a given state can obtain in the future and is updated by Eq. (5). The estimated Q value can be used to select actions that will yield higher value in the future.

$$Q(s_t, o_t) \leftarrow (1 - \alpha) \cdot Q(s_t, o_t) + \alpha \left(r_t + \gamma \cdot \max \left(Q \left(s_{t+1}, o' \right) \right) \right) \tag{5}$$

where s_t and a_t are the states (the swarm board in the case of THM) and behavior at time t, and r_t is the reward earned. $max(Q(s_{t+1}, o'))$ is the maximum Q value in the transition destination state, and this term is used to learn an action sequence that considers future rewards to be earned. α And γ are parameters for learning, called the learning rate and discount rate, respectively. A flowchart of Q learning is shown in Fig. 1.

Here, ε-greedy was employed for the agent's action selection. The agent randomly chooses an action with probability ε and chooses the action with the largest Q value with probability $(1 - \varepsilon)$.

3 Proposed Method

Because the BRT algorithm introduced in Sect. 2.2 is a trial-and-error search, even in environments that are new to the swarm, the swarm can find the optimal action options over time, as long as the action options are appropriate to the environment. However, they are unable to make use of this experience and thus cannot effectively adapt to similar environments. On the other hand, since the BRT algorithm agrees in advance which option to select and the number of agents has little impact on the consensus-building time, it is an algorithm that has a high potential to address the issues of non-stationarity and scalability of the environment.

Therefore, in this chapter, we propose QBRT, a learning BRT algorithm that introduces Q learning into the BRT agent and allows it to choose the best option more efficiently.

3.1 QBRT

The BRT algorithm introduced in Sect. 2.2 always randomly selects the next action $O_i(t + 1)$ from the remaining set of actions $(O - O_i(t))$ when agent A_i changes its option.

$$O_i(t + 1) \in O - O_i(t) \tag{6}$$

This may result in inefficient searches in some environments that have already been experienced. Therefore, QBRT adds an element of reinforcement learning to the part of the BRT agent's behavior that is changed to improve the efficiency of the search. Here, Q learning was chosen as the reinforcement learning method to be added. Here, agent A_i changes its options according to Eq. (7) instead of Eq. (6).

$$\begin{cases} O_i(t + 1) \in O - O_i(t) & probability \ (1 - \varepsilon_i) \\ O_i(t + 1) = \underset{o \in O(s_{t+1})}{argmax} \ Q_i(s_{t+1}, o) & probability \ \varepsilon_i \end{cases} \tag{7}$$

where s_t is the state of the environment observed by the swarm at time t, and $\underset{o \in O(s_{t+1})}{argmax} \ Q_i(s_{t+1}, o)$ is the maximum Q value of agent A_i in the transition destination environment. Here, the Q value of agent A_i is stored for each combination of observed environment state $S = s_l(l = 0 \sim L - 1)$ and option $O = o_m(m = 0 \sim M - 1)$ as in Eq. (8). L is the number of possible states of the environment.

$$Q_{i_{s_l,o_m}} = Q_i(s_l, o_m) \tag{8}$$

Agent A_i acts only when the swarm's option reaches a consensus state, and updates the Q value according to Eq. (4) in Sect. 2.2, regardless of whether the option is changed or not (Fig. 2(10)). On the other hand, if the swarm does not consent, it does not act and re-selects (Eq. (9)). The reward r_i given in process (9) in Fig. 2 is set by the designer to an appropriate reward for the goal state (final board in THM). This allows each agent in the swarm to act and learn only when it makes the same options as the other agents, thus acting and learning cohesively as a swarm. As a result, if enough exploration and learning takes place, the swarm can obtain Q values through trial-and-error iterations with the environment to obtain an optimal series of options.

$$\begin{cases} execution & \exists j, \forall i, O_i(t) = o_j \\ reselection & otherwise \end{cases} \tag{9}$$

A conceptual diagram of the proposed method is shown in Fig. 2. In the traditional BRT algorithm, when changing options, the only change is random, whereas the learning BRT algorithm adds a Q learning component to each agent (Fig. 2(6), (9), (10)).

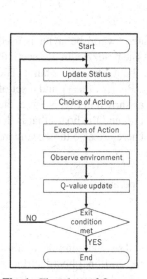

Fig. 1. Flowchart of Q learning

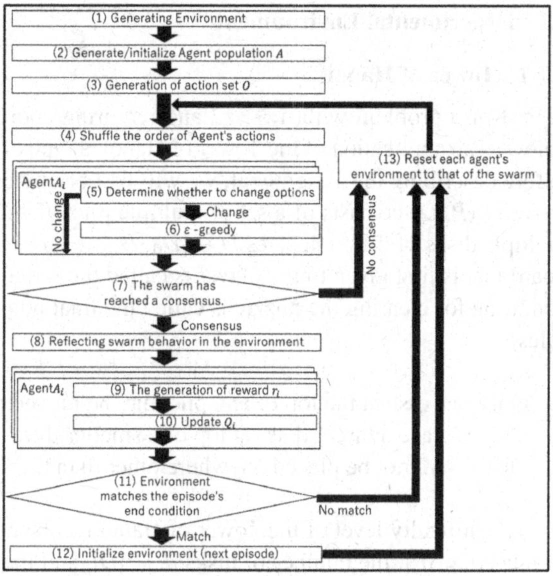

Fig. 2. Conceptual diagram of QBRT

3.2 Behavior of Swarms Implementing QBRT

The agent implementing the QBRT proposed here observes the state of the environment (the THM board) and presents the options it wishes to execute to the swarm as a whole. Then, only when all the agents' presentations agree on one option, i.e., when the swarm has reached a consensus state, does the swarm actually act and the agents learn. Therefore, each agent acts and learns by incorporating the actions of other agents, so that the entire swarm behaves like a single agent, making the algorithm capable of dealing with the non-stationarity of the environment. In addition, because it is based on the BRT algorithm, the time required to reach a consensus state does not change significantly even when the number of agents increases, so it can generally be said to address scalability issues.

In Sect. 4, as a first step to verify the above, THM, as a cooperative problem for swarms, is run on a swarm that implements QBRT.

4   Experiments

This chapter first describes the environment of the experiment, Tower of Hanoi by Multiagent (hereafter, THM). Next, we will verify the effectiveness of the QBRT by conducting computer experiments playing THM with each of the conventional BRT algorithm and QBRT, which adds Q learning to the BRT algorithm.

4.1 Experimental Environment

4.1.1 Tower of Hanoi

A best-of-n problem with n $>>$ 2 and requiring coordinated swarm behavior is used below as an application of the Tower of Hanoi, a type of classical puzzle. In this section, before describing the assignment, we will first briefly describe the tower of Hanoi. The puzzle $T(P, D)$ consists of a set of multiple piles $P \in \{P_0, P_1, \ldots, P_{p-1}\}$ and a set of multiple disks of different sizes $D \in \{D_0, D_1, \ldots, D_{d-1}\}$, as shown in Fig. 3. Here, the board that is first given to the player is called the initial board, and the board that is the condition for clearing the puzzle is called the final board. There are also three standard rules,

1. Only one disc at the top of any pile may be moved per operation.
2. Do not place a larger disk on top of a smaller disk.
3. Disks shall not be placed anywhere other than the stakes.

The difficulty level of the Tower of Hanoi can be adjusted by changing the number of piles $p = |P|$, the number of disks $d = |D|$, and the initial and final board surfaces, and it is generally known that the larger p, the lower the difficulty level and the larger d, the higher the difficulty level.

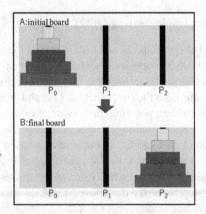

Fig. 3. Tower of Hanoi: Example of $T(3, 5)$

4.1.2 THM: The Tower of Hanoi Multi-agent

Tower of Hanoi is essentially a puzzle game played by a single player; to make it playable by a large number of agents, the following changes were made. In the following, this is referred to as THM (Tower of Hanoi by Multiagent). First, THM prepares a pair of Hanoi towers (Fig. 4(1)). Each agent in the swarm then observes the current board (Fig. 4(2)) and decides which disc to move next and where to move it (Fig. 4(3)). This is the move of agent A_i. Next, the moves of all agents are counted, and if all agents agree on a move, the board reflects the move accordingly as a "swarm consensus" (Fig. 4(4)). The disc moves to select a move on a new board (Fig. 4(5)). On the other hand, if the hands of all agents do not match, the board of the Tower of Hanoi is not changed. However, time elapses, and again all agents re-determine their moves (left-pointing arrows in Fig. 4(3)).

Since we want to prototype a concise BRT agent that performs Q learning, we evaluated the board only when the board changed. If the BRT agent's action is in a non-consensus state, the board is not evaluated.

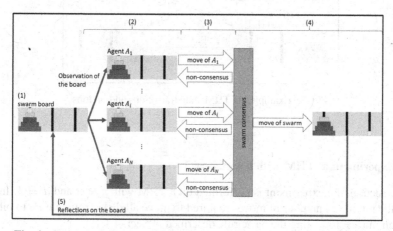

Fig. 4. Conceptual diagram of the execution of the Tower of Hanoi as a swarm

4.1.3 THM Settings

In the experiments conducted in this chapter, the number of piles is p and the number of disks is d. In THM, the state of reinforcement learning corresponds to the board, the state set S is $\{s_0, \ldots, s_{p^d-1}\}$ and the action set O is $\{o_0, \ldots, o_{p \cdot (p-1)-1}\}$. The initial board was unified with all disks at pile P_0 on the left side as shown in Fig. 3A, and the final board was unified with all disks at pile P_2 on the right side as shown in Fig. 3B. The total number of possible states $|S|$ is p^d and the number of elements of the action set $|O|$ is $p \cdot (p-1)$.

Figure 5 shows an example of the state transition of the THM board S observed by the swarm for $p = 3$, $d = 5$, and option O. If option o_1 (move the disk from pile P_0 to pile P_2), which can move the disk in state s_0 of the board, is executed, the state transitions from s_0 to s_1. If an option that cannot move the disk in state s_0 (e.g., o_2 (move the disk from pile P_1 to pile P_0)) is executed, the state is treated as a transition from s_0 to s_0. However, the agent shall not know in advance whether any of the options can move the disk in a given state.

The series of trials from the initial board to the final board is referred to as an episode in the following. When the Tower of Hanoi moves to the final board, the board is initialized and the next episode begins.

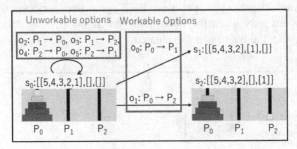

Fig. 5. Examples of THM state transitions and options

4.2 Experiment at THM with $p = 3, d = 3$

In this section, the experiment is performed on a THM with $p = 3$ and $d = 3$. In this case, the minimum number of moves required to move all disks from pile P_0 to pile P_2 is seven moves, following the basic rule described in Sect. 4.1.1.

4.2.1 Performing THM with the Conventional BRT Algorithm

To compare with QBRT, we first run the THM with the conventional BRT algorithm.

The number of agents N of the BRT algorithm treated in this section is set to 30. Also, the number of options O, M, is $p \cdot (p - 1)$ (disks from P_0 to P_1, ..., from P_0 to P_{p-1}, ..., from P_{p-1} to P_0, ..., from P_{p-1} to P_{p-2}).

According to these conditions, the results of 40 episodes of THM run by the conventional BRT algorithm are shown in Fig. 6.

A run with the conventional BRT algorithm, which agrees on nearly random options, resulted in a maximum of 1394 moves, a minimum of 21 moves, and an average of 302.1 moves. The number of moves required to complete an episode was significantly greater than the minimum number of moves is seven, and there was no tendency for the number of moves to shorten as the episodes were repeated. The average number of non-consensus moves per move, which is the time it takes to reach an agreement, was 532.1.

4.2.2 Performing THM with QBRT

The setting of the number of options M in the QBRT is the same as in Sect. 4.2.1. However, each agent has its Q_i value, learning rate α_i, discount rate γ_i, and random learning rate ε_i, since it selects itself according to Eq. (6) proposed in Sect. 3. Each agent acts collectively as a swarm using the BRT algorithm, but because no two individuals are the same in the real world, each agent receives the results differently. To reproduce and verify this, we conducted experiments with swarms in which the parameters α_i, γ_i, and ε_i were set randomly and the agents differed individually, and with swarms in which all the parameters were unified to simplify the experiment and no individual differences were observed. Here, α_i, γ_i, and ε_i are assumed to be randomly determined by a Gaussian distribution with mean 0.5 and variance 0.5/3, with each value greater than 0 and less than 1 and a bell-shaped distribution. The rewards for each Q learning were set as shown in Table 1. The "workable options" in the table are those options that can move the disks. On the other hand, "unworkable options" are those options that cannot move the disk. It also gives a large positive reward to the swarm if it chooses the "option to reach the final state" and it is carried out.

Table 1. Setting Rewards for Q-learning at THM with $p = 3, d = 3$

Options	Workable options	unworkable options	Option to reach the final state
Rewards	0	0	1000

Furthermore, agent A_i in QBRT has variables as shown in Table.2

Table 2. Variables and initial values of agent A_i in QBRT

Variable name	Description	Initial value
τ	Constant indicating predicted increase in support	$0.01/M$
t_{last}	Time of last option change	0
O	Possible options	$O \in \{o_0, ..., o_{p \cdot (p-1)-1}\}$
Q_i	Q-table for Q-learning	0
α_i	Q-learning learning rate	Randomly determined by Gaussian distribution with mean 0.5 and variance 0.5/3
γ_i	Q-learning discount rate	
ε_i	Probability of randomly choosing an option in ε-greedy	

The Hanoi tower was run for 40 episodes with four QBRT combinations of individual differences in swarms with $N = 30$ and 100 agents, according to the above conditions. These are summarized in Fig. 7.

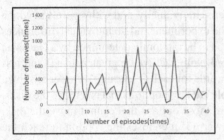
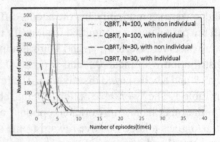

Fig. 6. Results of running conventional BRT algorithm on THM with $p = 3, d = 3$

Fig. 7. Results of running the QBRT algorithm on THM with $p = 3, d = 3$ (Color figure online)

All QBRT swarms are now able to finish an episode in 7 moves, the shortest number of moves within 10 episodes. In all conditions, the number of moves was significantly reduced from the average of runs with the conventional BRT algorithm. The average number of non-consensus moves per swarm consensus, which is the time it takes to reach consensus, is 500.9 for the swarm with $N = 100$ non-individual differences (yellow dashed line in Fig. 7), 505.4 for the swarm with $N = 100$ individual differences (red dashed line in Fig. 7), 513.4 for the swarm with $N = 30$ non-individual differences (green dashed line in Fig. 7), 539.4 for the swarm with $N = 30$ individual differences (the blue straight line in Fig. 7), which is about the same as the number of swarms executed by the conventional BRT or slightly reduced. This is presumably because learning has made it easier for the agent to select certain options.

These results suggest that the same trend would be true even if the number of agents is further increased, and thus QBRT was able to improve the non-stationarity and scalability problems to some extent regardless of the number of agents.

4.3   Experiment at THM with $p = 3, d = 5$

In this section, the experiment is performed on a THM with $p = 3$ and $d = 3$. In this case, the minimum number of moves required to move all disks from pile P_0 to pile P_2 is 31 moves, following the basic rule described in Sect. 2.5.1.

4.3.1   Performing THM with the Conventional BRT Algorithm

To compare with QBRT, we first run the THM with the conventional BRT algorithm. The settings for the number of agents N and the number of options O, M, are the same as in Sect. 4.2.1.

According to these conditions, the results of 40 episodes of THM run by the conventional BRT algorithm are shown in Fig. 8.

A run with the conventional BRT algorithm, which agrees on nearly random choices, resulted in a maximum of 13372 moves, a minimum of 579 moves, and an average of 4142.2 moves. The number of moves required to complete an episode was significantly greater than the minimum number of moves, 31, and as with Sect. 4.2.1, there was no tendency for the number of moves to shorten over the course of the episode.

4.3.2 Performing THM with QBRT

The variable settings for the number of options M and agent A_i in the QBRT are the same as in Sect. 4.2.2. The number of agents $N = 30$ and the rewards for each Q learning were set as shown in Table 3. The "workable options" in the table are those options that can move the disks. On the other hand, "unworkable options" are those options that cannot move the disk. It also gives a large positive reward to the swarm if it chooses the "option to reach the final state" and it is carried out. Also, experiment with negative rewards for swarms with the intention of speeding up learning.

Table 3. Setting Rewards for Q-learning at THM with $p = 3, d = 5$

	Options	Workable options	unworkable options	Option to reach the final state
Rewards	No Negative Reward	0	0	1000
	Negative Reward	−0.1	−100000	1000

According to these conditions, 250 episodes of the Tower of Hanoi were run by QBRT with four different combinations of individual differences and negative rewards. These are summarized in Fig. 9.

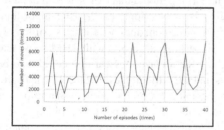

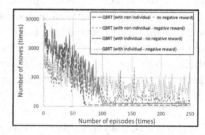

Fig. 8. Results of running conventional BRT algorithm on THM with $p = 3, d = 5$

Fig. 9. Results of running the QBRT algorithm on THM with $p = 3, d = 5$ (Color figure online)

In the QBRT with non-individual differences and no negative reward (Fig. 9 green dashed line), it took 34 moves in about 70 episodes from the beginning of the experiment, and in the QBRT with individual differences and no negative reward (Fig. 9 yellow dashed line), it took 39 moves in about 100 episodes from the beginning of the experiment. Episodes could be completed. In the QBRT with non-individual differences and with negative rewards (Fig. 9 red dashed line), the shortest number of moves, 31, appeared in the first 115 episodes of the experiment, and since then the episode has been completed in the shortest number of moves several times. Q learning also allowed for a significant reduction from the average of runs using the conventional BRT algorithm in all conditions, provided that sufficient learning had progressed.

In the runs with swarms with no negative rewards (Fig. 9 green dashed line and red dashed line), learning stopped when the shortest number of moves was not found, but this is thought to be because once some better series are found, positive rewards continue to be given to that series, which prevents further search for better series. On the other hand, in the runs with swarms with negative reward (Fig. 9 dashed yellow line and solid blue line), the search in the initial phase progressed more efficiently than those with no negative reward, so we can expect the learning to proceed even faster and more consistently if the negative reward is adjusted.

This experiment confirmed that QBRT is able to solve the puzzle even as the THM difficulty level increases. It was also more efficient than the BRT algorithm in solving the cooperative problem where all agents make the same move. Since QBRT is based on the BRT algorithm, which has the property that the time required for agreement does not change significantly as the number of agents increases, the learning speed is not expected to change significantly even if it is run with a larger number of agents. Therefore, we were able to implement a learning algorithm that solves the problems of non-stationarity and scalability in the cooperative problem. On the other hand, the issue of competition is unknown. Therefore, it is necessary to verify in the future whether QBRT is effective against the contention problem and whether it works without problems even when executed with a large number of agents.

5 Conclusion

Here, we proposed QBRT as a reinforcement learning model that can deal with the non-stationarity of the environment and scalability issues by applying the BRT algorithm, which has the property that the time required for agreement does not change significantly even when the number of agents increases. Experimental results with THM show that QBRT solves puzzles more quickly than the BRT algorithm. Learning could also be advanced by increasing the number of agents and the difficulty level of the THM. Therefore, it can be said that we were able to implement a learning algorithm that improves non-stationarity and scalability issues to some extent in the cooperative problem. In the future, it is necessary to verify whether QBRT is also effective for competing problems where the number of agents increases or agents move differently.

References

1. Canese, L., et al.: Multi-agent reinforcement learning: a review of challenges and applications. Appl. Sci. 11(11), 4948 (2021)
2. Wang, Y., Damani, M., Wang, P., Cao, Y., Sartoretti, G.: Distributed reinforcement learning for robot teams: a review. arXiv preprint arXiv:2204.03516 (2022)
3. Matta, M., et al.: Q-RTS: a real-time swarm intelligence based on multi-agent Q-learning. Electron. Lett. 55(10), 589–591 (2019)
4. Matignon, L., Laurent, G.J., Le Fort-Piat, N.: Hysteretic q-learning: an algorithm for decentralized reinforcement learning in cooperative multi-agent teams. In: 2007 IEEE/RSJ International Conference on Intelligent Robots and Systems, pp. 64–69. IEEE (2007)

5. Qu, G., Lin, Y., Wierman, A., Li, N.: Scalable multi-agent reinforcement learning for networked systems with average reward. Adv. Neural. Inf. Process. Syst. **33**, 2074–2086 (2020)
6. Kar, S., Moura, J.M., Poor, H.V.: QD-learning: a collaborative distributed strategy for multi-agent reinforcement learning through consensus + innovations. IEEE Trans. Signal Process. **61**(7), 1848–1862 (2013)
7. Palmer, G., Tuyls, K., Bloembergen, D., Savani, R.: Lenient multi-agent deep reinforcement learning. arXiv preprint arXiv:1707.04402 (2017)
8. Phung, N.H., Kubo, M., Sato, H.: El Farol Bar problem by agreement algorithm based on trial and error behavior at the macro lever. In: Proceedings of the 22nd Asia Pacific Symposium on Intelligent and Evolutionary Systems (2018)
9. Valentini, G., Ferrante, E., Dorigo, M.: The best-of-n problem in robot swarms: formalization, state of the art, and novel perspectives. Front. Robot. AI **4**, 9 (2017)

A Study on Effectiveness of BERT Models and Task-Conditioned Reasoning Strategy for Medical Visual Question Answering

Chau Nguyen[1(✉)], Tung Le[2], Nguyen-Khang Le[1], Trung-Tin Pham[1], and Le-Minh Nguyen[1]

[1] Japan Advanced Institute of Science and Technology, Nomi, Japan
{chau.nguyen,lnkhang,tinpham,nguyenml}@jaist.ac.jp
[2] University of Science - VNUHCM, Ho Chi Minh City, Vietnam
lttung@fit.hcmus.edu.vn

Abstract. Medical visual question answering task requires a framework to understand a medical question in natural language and examine the corresponding image to produce the answer to the question. The common framework consists of a language understanding module, a visual understanding module, a signal fusion module, and an answer prediction module. Most existing works employed recurrent neural network-based models for the language understanding module. However, these approaches may not produce robust text presentations and are hard to interpret. On the other hand, BERT models are more robust for text representation and can provide a clue for interpretability via the attention weights between the words. Besides, as the questions consist of closed-answer questions and open-answer questions, the task-conditioned reasoning strategy was proposed to handle each type of question separately while maintaining several modules in the framework to be shared. In this paper, we investigate the effectiveness of pre-trained BERT models and the task-conditioned reasoning strategy for the task of medical visual question answering on the VQA-RAD dataset. Experimental results demonstrate improvements when pre-trained BERT models are combined with the task-conditioned reasoning strategy.

Keywords: Medical visual question answering · Visual question answering · Task-conditioned reasoning · Conditional reasoning

1 Introduction

Medical visual question answering (medical VQA) is the task aiming to answer a natural language question on a medical image. Medical VQA requires a system to understand the natural language in the medical context (i.e., understand the question) as well as to pay attention to the areas in the image that contain the clues for the answer, then produce an answer based on the knowledge from both language signals and visual signals. The common framework consists of a

Y. Kambayashi et al. (Eds.): AICON 2022, LNICST 477, pp. 60–71, 2023.
https://doi.org/10.1007/978-3-031-29126-5_5

language understanding module, a visual understanding module, a signal fusion module, and an answer prediction module (see Fig. 1). In fact, medical VQA is a generation task. However, most existing systems [6,7,18,19,23,24] consider it as a classification task (i.e., the answer prediction module is an answer classifier where the set of answers is a collection of answers from the training set).

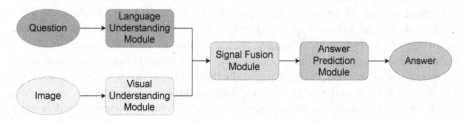

Fig. 1. The common framework for medical VQA

CMSA-MTPT [7] was proposed as a multi-task pre-training technique where the visual understanding module (which are ResNet [10] models) are pre-trained in a way that is compatible with the language understanding module (which is an LSTM (long short-term memory [12]) model). While LSTM is trained from scratch, BERT [5] models can be pre-trained so that the learned language patterns can be leveraged during the fine-tuning phase. In fact, BERT has become one of the dominant language embedders in the field of natural language processing (NLP). Besides, the attention weights between the words provided by BERT models also give a clue for the researcher for interpretability or for error analysis. Hence, employing BERT models as the language understanding module should strengthen the framework. [23] proposed task-conditioned reasoning (TCR) strategy which addresses different types of questions separately.

In our study, we replace LSTM in the CMSA-MTPT framework with pre-trained BERT models (BERT [5] and BioBERT [17] in particular) and apply the TCR strategy to this framework. We did experiments with many settings to investigate the effectiveness of pre-trained BERT models and TCR for the medical VQA task.

Table 1. Statistics on the dataset

Data split	Train	Test
# questions	3064	451
# questions with closed answer	1821	272
# questions with open answer	1243	179
# different answers	458	83
# different closed answers	56	13
# different open answers	431	77
# overlapped closed & open answers	29	7

2   Related Work

2.1   VQA-RAD Dataset

Among many medical VQA datasets [1–3,9,11,15,16], VQA-RAD [16] is popular as it is the only dataset which contains natural questions on a variety types of questions. Table 1 provides some statistics on the VQA-RAD dataset. The training data contains 3064 questions while the test data contains 451 questions on a total of 315 radiological images. The question set includes questions about plane, modality, organ system, abnormality, object/condition presence, position, color, size, attribute other, counting, and others. The answers to those questions are divided into closed questions (i.e., limited-choice questions such as yes/no or left/right) and open questions (i.e., non-limited-choice questions which may have multiple correct answers). The radiological images are images of the head, chest, and abdomen areas.

2.2   CMSA-MTPT Framework

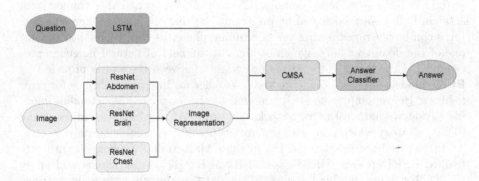

Fig. 2. The CMSA-MTPT framework

The CMSA-MTPT framework (Fig. 2) followed the common framework described above. Experiments were performed on the VQA-RAD dataset. This framework used LSTM as the language understanding module and employed pre-trained ResNet models as the visual understanding module. A cross-modal self-attention module (CMSA) is proposed as the signal fusion module, which outperforms SAN [22] and BAN [14]. The answer prediction module (answer classifier) is a simple 2-layer MLP (multi-layer perceptron) classifier. Because of the lack of training images in the VQA-RAD dataset (only 315 radiological images of 3 areas: head, chest, abdomen), it is impractical to apply state-of-the-art models in VQA [4,13] directly to medical VQA. CMSA-MTPT leveraged different available image datasets for each area for pre-training corresponding ResNet models, in a transfer learning manner [18,20]. Each ResNet model is designed to embed the content of an image type (head, chest, or abdomen). Given a medical image, the 3 ResNet models will generate 3 vectors representing it. The final representation of the image is a soft combination of the 3 vectors based on an image type classifier.

Because of the labels provided for those external data, ResNet models for the head and chest are trained on a classification task while the ResNet model for the abdomen is trained on the image segmentation task. Besides, CMSA-MTPT also proposed a multi-task pre-training strategy so that the compatibility of the pre-trained ResNet models and the language understanding module is ensured. Specifically, the loss function for pre-training ResNet models not only contains classification/segmentation loss but also contains a loss specifying the compatibility score between the type of the image and the language representation of the input question. For the signal fusion module, the CMSA-MTPT framework proposed cross-modal self-attention (CMSA) to effectively fuse the representation of the question and the image (see Fig. 2).

2.3   Task-Condition Reasoning Strategy

The main idea of task-condition reasoning (TCR) [23] is to have two signal fusion modules and two answer prediction modules to handle closed-answer questions and open-answer questions separately while other modules (i.e., language understanding module and visual understanding module) are shared.

3   Our Framework

3.1   Overview

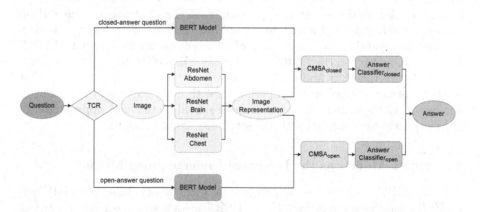

Fig. 3. An overview of our framework

Figure 3 provides an overview of our framework. Our framework is based on the CMSA-MTPT framework [7]. The two main adjustments are (i) to enhance the language understanding module (replacing LSTM with BERT models: BERT [5] and BioBERT [17]) and (ii) to employ the task-conditioned reasoning strategy [23].

Intuitively, BERT models (especially BioBERT - which is pre-trained on the corpora of the medical domain) are pre-trained on huge text corpora, which is supposed to adapt promptly to understand natural language in medical fields. Besides, as BERT deploys the self-attention architecture, the attention weights between the words can be leveraged as a clue for error analysis and interpretability of the model.

Table 2. Length of the questions by different tokenizers

Data split	Value	Word tokenizer (# words)	BERT tokenizer (# tokens)	BioBERT tokenizer (# tokens)
Train	max	21	28	28
	min	3	5	6
	average	6.43	11.76	12.06
	median	6	11	11
Test	max	22	32	33
	min	3	5	6
	average	6.89	11.51	11.88
	median	7	11	11

Table 2 contains the information about the length of the questions by different tokenizers: word tokenizer, BERT tokenizer, and BioBERT tokenizer. On average, the length (by words) of a question is less than 7 although some of them can reach the length of 22 words. In the original CMSA-MTPT framework, they truncate the question to a maximum of 12 words before feeding it to LSTM. In our case, as we use the BERT tokenizer and BioBERT tokenizer, the average number of tokens is around 12 tokens while there are some questions that reach 33 tokens. We performed experiments with many values of the maximum number of tokens to investigate which value should be the most appropriate. In particular, we experimented with the set 12, 20, 25, 30, and 40.

3.2 BERT Models as the Language Understanding Module

For the BERT models, we experimented with BERT base uncased[1] and BioBERT base cased version 1.2[2]. As BERT models contain a big number of trainable parameters, fine-tuning all those parameters makes the training process longer. Hence, for each BERT model, we tried with 2 settings: (i) frozen

---

[1] https://huggingface.co/bert-base-uncased.
[2] https://huggingface.co/dmis-lab/biobert-base-cased-v1.2.

BERT model: freeze all BERT layers and only use the BERT model as a frozen text embedder, and (ii) unfrozen BERT model: freeze all BERT layers except for the last one (i.e., only the parameters of the last layer of BERT model are trained along with other modules).

The attention weights provided BERT models in different heads demonstrate behaviors which seems to be related to the sentence's structure [21]. Although those behaviors are not fully investigated, they still provide a clue to determine how the model may work. Figure 4 shows an example of a visualization of a head produced by a BERT model (see Fig. 4).

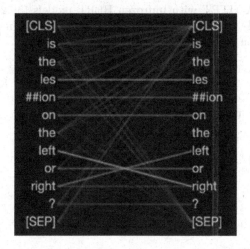

Fig. 4. Visualization of the attention weights of layer 2's head 12

3.3 Setting of the Task-Conditioned Strategy

Previous frameworks [6,7,18] trained a fusion module to learn the fused representation of all samples and classified to 458 answers (458 is the number of different answers in the training data, see Table 1). However, TCR first determines the type of the question (question with closed answer or question with open answer), then employs a model to learn the fusion of each type before feeding it into the answer classifiers. Here, the answer classifier for closed-answer questions has only 56 classes and the answer classifier for open-answer questions has 431 classes. There are 29 overlapped answers between the two sets.

4 Experiments

4.1 Training ResNet Models

As mentioned above, the ResNet models are trained so that they are compatible with the corresponding language understanding module. Because in our case, we replace LSTM with BERT models, so we also need to re-train the corresponding ResNet models for the BERT models. Table 3 shows the experimental results. As mentioned above, all models are trained not only with a loss function indicating the compatibility of the image and the corresponding question, but also be trained with another task (a segmentation task for abdomen data and a classification task for brain data and chest data). We train each model for 200 epochs.

As shown in Table 3, we can roughly reproduce the ResNet models for the CMSA-MTPT with LSTM. The other experiments on CMSA-MTPT with BERT models demonstrate the same results in most cases, except for the compatibility accuracy of CMSA-MTPT with unfrozen BERT models (59.26% compared to 78.70% as reported). It may be because, with unfrozen BERT models, the models need to fine-tune on more parameters.

Table 3. Results of ResNet models for the CMSA-MTPT with LSTM. *Comp. acc.* means compatibility accuracy. *Cls. acc.* means classification accuracy. Values in **bold** indicate the highest values in the columns.

Model	Max words/max tokens	Abdomen data		Brain data		Chest data	
		mIOU	Comp. acc.	Cls. acc.	Comp. acc.	Cls. acc.	Comp. acc.
CMSA-MTPT with LSTM (reported)	12	71.00	78.70	98.40	89.10	98.70	83.60
CMSA-MTPT with LSTM (reproduced)	12	81.98	73.15	**100.00**	90.62	97.84	86.21
CMSA-MTPT with frozen BERT base	12	77.02	78.70	98.44	90.62	96.55	86.21
	20	76.73	79.63	96.88	90.62	96.55	87.93
	25	74.22	75.00	96.88	90.62	96.98	**90.09**
	30	75.88	77.78	98.44	90.62	97.84	88.79
	40	73.06	75.00	98.44	87.50	96.12	87.07
CMSA-MTPT with unfrozen BERT base	12	74.23	81.48	98.44	78.12	98.71	62.93
	20	82.58	59.26	**100.00**	78.12	98.71	62.93
	25	**83.32**	59.26	98.44	78.12	98.71	62.93
	30	82.44	59.26	98.44	78.12	**99.14**	62.93
	40	81.66	59.26	98.44	78.12	**99.14**	62.93
CMSA-MTPT with frozen BioBERT base	12	71.15	77.78	96.88	**96.88**	96.55	85.78
	20	74.31	75.93	96.88	93.75	97.41	86.21
	25	69.58	78.70	98.44	95.31	98.28	86.21
	30	72.71	82.41	96.88	89.06	98.28	87.07
	40	73.21	**83.33**	95.31	95.31	97.84	86.64
CMSA-MTPT with unfrozen BioBERT base	12	82.90	59.26	98.44	78.12	98.71	86.21
	20	82.38	59.26	**100.00**	78.12	96.98	88.79
	25	76.03	78.70	96.88	78.12	98.28	62.93
	30	83.03	59.26	**100.00**	78.12	97.84	89.66
	40	82.89	59.26	98.44	78.12	98.28	89.66

4.2   CMSA-MTPT with BERT Models

Experimental Settings. We did experiments on the VQA-RAD dataset. Each model is trained on an NVIDIA A40 GPU. Table 4 shows the experimental settings. Following [7], we also apply warmup steps [8]. We train for 250 epochs.

Results. Table 5 shows the experimental results. Here, "Open" means model accuracy on only open-answer questions, "Closed" means model accuracy on

Table 4. Parameter settings

Parameter	Value
# epochs	250
initial learning rate (LR)	0.005
LR decay step	48
LR decay rate	0.75
batch size	32

Table 5. Results of CMSA-MTPT with BERT models. Values in **bold** indicate the highest values in the columns.

Model	Max words/max tokens	Accuracy		
		Open	Closed	All
CMSA-MTPT with LSTM (reproduced)	12	61.45	77.21	70.95
CMSA-MTPT with frozen BERT base	12	50.84	78.31	67.41
	20	54.75	76.47	67.85
	25	59.22	80.15	71.84
	30	56.42	75.74	68.07
	40	57.54	80.51	71.40
CMSA-MTPT with unfrozen BERT base	12	60.34	79.41	71.84
	20	60.34	79.04	71.62
	25	60.34	80.51	**72.51**
	30	58.10	77.57	69.84
	40	57.54	77.57	69.62
CMSA-MTPT with frozen BioBERT base	12	53.63	77.21	67.85
	20	56.98	80.15	70.95
	25	61.45	79.78	**72.51**
	30	59.22	**80.88**	72.28
	40	59.22	79.04	71.18
CMSA-MTPT with unfrozen BioBERT base	12	60.89	79.41	72.06
	20	**62.01**	76.84	70.95
	25	60.34	78.31	71.18
	30	59.78	78.68	71.18
	40	59.22	76.47	69.62

only closed-answer questions, and "All" means model accuracy on all questions. While the reported accuracy is 73.17%, our reproduced accuracy is only 70.95%. We compare the reproduced accuracy with our methods.

The experimental results show that the CMSA-MTPT model with unfrozen BERT base and the CMSA-MTPT model with frozen BioBERT base produce the highest accuracy on the whole test set with 72.51%. There is an improvement of 1.56% (from 70.95% to 72.51%) when replacing the LSTM language understanding module with a BERT model.

4.3   Task-Conditioned Reasoning CMSA-MTPT with BERT Models

We use the same settings as in training CMSA-MTPT with BERT models. Table 6 shows the experimental results when applying the task-condition reasoning strategy on CMSA-MTPT with BERT models. TCR helps improve the accuracy to 73.17% on the setting of TCR CMSA-MTPT with frozen BioBERT base.

Table 6. Results of TCR CMSA-MTPT with BERT models. Values in **bold** indicate the highest values in the columns.

Model	Max words/ max tokens	Accuracy		
		Open	Closed	All
TCR CMSA-MTPT with frozen BERT base	12	51.96	79.41	68.51
	20	53.07	79.41	68.96
	25	53.07	80.51	69.62
	30	60.34	78.68	71.40
	40	53.07	76.10	66.96
TCR CMSA-MTPT with unfrozen BERT base	12	61.45	79.04	72.06
	20	61.45	77.21	70.95
	25	58.66	77.21	69.84
	30	59.78	78.68	71.18
	40	58.10	77.94	70.07
TCR CMSA-MTPT with frozen BioBERT base	12	55.31	81.99	71.40
	20	59.22	79.78	71.62
	25	62.01	79.04	72.28
	30	58.66	**82.72**	**73.17**
	40	52.51	81.62	70.07
TCR CMSA-MTPT with unfrozen BioBERT base	12	59.78	79.04	71.40
	20	**62.57**	77.57	71.62
	25	60.89	76.10	70.07
	30	60.34	81.25	72.95
	40	55.31	77.94	68.96

TCR is helpful because it can separately train different modules for different types of questions where the answer classifiers need to deal with fewer classifiers: instead of dealing with 458 classes, the closed-answer classifier only deals with 56 classes, and the open-answer classifier deals with 431 classes (Table 1). Table 1 also shows that the number of answers in the test set is much fewer than those in the training set: 13 different closed answers and 77 different open answers. Hence, we tried an experiment where the models are only trained with the answer set in the test set instead of the answer set in the training set. It is an "oracle" setting so that we can see how the models perform if they are only trained on the questions that have the answers in the answer set of test data. Table 7 shows the results of this experiment.

The highest oracle performance is achieved with 76.72% by the oracle TCR CMSA-MTPT with frozen BioBERT base model with the max tokens set to 40. This model has significantly improved the accuracy of answering open-answer questions (increase 6.15%, from 62.57% to 68.72%). However, the accuracy on

Table 7. Results of oracle TCR CMSA-MTPT with BERT models. Values in **bold** indicate the highest values in the columns.

Model	Max words/max tokens	Accuracy		
		Open	Closed	All
Oracle TCR CMSA-MTPT with frozen BERT base	12	58.10	79.78	71.18
	20	60.34	79.41	71.84
	25	62.01	77.21	71.18
	30	60.89	81.25	73.17
	40	64.25	79.04	73.17
Oracle TCR CMSA-MTPT with unfrozen BERT base	12	64.25	79.41	73.39
	20	64.25	81.62	74.72
	25	63.69	80.88	74.06
	30	62.01	77.94	71.62
	40	62.01	79.04	72.28
Oracle TCR CMSA-MTPT with frozen BioBERT base	12	60.34	77.57	70.73
	20	63.13	79.78	73.17
	25	62.01	81.62	73.84
	30	63.69	81.62	74.50
	40	**68.72**	**81.99**	**76.72**
Oracle TCR CMSA-MTPT with unfrozen BioBERT base	12	60.89	80.88	72.95
	20	64.25	77.57	72.28
	25	64.25	79.04	73.17
	30	60.89	79.78	72.28
	40	64.80	76.84	72.06

closed-answer questions decreases minorly. These observations indicate that the future model should focus more on open-answer questions as its accuracy is still low and can be increased significantly.

4.4 A Clue for Interpretability in BERT Models

Figure 4 shows the visualization of the attention weights of layer 2's head 12 for the question *"is the lesion on the left or right?"*. The model chosen for visualization is the BioBERT model in the TCR CMSA-MTPT model with frozen BioBERT base (max tokens = 30). In this closed-answer question, the answer should be *left* or *right*. As shown in Fig. 4, while many tokens (i.e., *les*, *##ion*, *on*) focus the most on itself, the token *left* focus the most on token *right*, and *vice versa*. It may indicate that this head learned the pattern of extracting the answer from the similar question in the training dataset.

5 Conclusion

In this paper, we investigate the effectiveness of pre-trained BERT models and the task-conditioned reasoning strategy for the task of medical visual question answering on the VQA-RAD dataset. Via comprehensive experiments, it is demonstrated that pre-trained BERT models (i.e., BERT base and BioBERT base) are suitable for this task and can replace LSTM as the language understanding module. Besides, the task-conditioned reasoning strategy also demonstrates improvements when employed in the framework. It is suggested that future research should focus more on the open-answer questions.

References

1. Abacha, A.B., Datla, V.V., Hasan, S.A., Demner-Fushman, D., Müller, H.: Overview of the VQA-med task at ImageCLEF 2020: visual question answering and generation in the medical domain. In: CLEF (Working Notes) (2020)
2. Abacha, A.B., Hasan, S.A., Datla, V.V., Liu, J., Demner-Fushman, D., Müller, H.: VQA-med: overview of the medical visual question answering task at ImageCLEF 2019. In: CLEF (Working Notes), vol. 2 (2019)
3. Allaouzi, I., Ahmed, M.B., Benamrou, B.: An encoder-decoder model for visual question answering in the medical domain. In: CLEF (Working Notes) (2019)
4. Anderson, P., et al.: Bottom-up and top-down attention for image captioning and visual question answering. In: Proceedings of the IEEE Conference on Computer Vision and Pattern Recognition, pp. 6077–6086 (2018)
5. Devlin, J., Chang, M.W., Lee, K., Toutanova, K.: BERT: pre-training of deep bidirectional transformers for language understanding. arXiv preprint arXiv:1810.04805 (2018)
6. Do, T., Nguyen, B.X., Tjiputra, E., Tran, M., Tran, Q.D., Nguyen, A.: Multiple meta-model quantifying for medical visual question answering. In: de Bruijne, M., et al. (eds.) MICCAI 2021. LNCS, vol. 12905, pp. 64–74. Springer, Cham (2021). https://doi.org/10.1007/978-3-030-87240-3_7

7. Gong, H., Chen, G., Liu, S., Yu, Y., Li, G.: Cross-modal self-attention with multi-task pre-training for medical visual question answering. In: Proceedings of the 2021 International Conference on Multimedia Retrieval, pp. 456–460 (2021)

8. Goyal, P., et al.: Accurate, large minibatch SGD: training imagenet in 1 hour. arXiv preprint arXiv:1706.02677 (2017)

9. Hasan, S.A., Ling, Y., Farri, O., Liu, J., Müller, H., Lungren, M.: Overview of ImageCLEF 2018 medical domain visual question answering task. Technical report, 10–14 September 2018 (2018)

10. He, K., Zhang, X., Ren, S., Sun, J.: Deep residual learning for image recognition. In: Proceedings of the IEEE Conference on Computer Vision and Pattern Recognition, pp. 770–778 (2016)

11. He, X., Zhang, Y., Mou, L., Xing, E., Xie, P.: PathVQA: 30000+ questions for medical visual question answering. arXiv preprint arXiv:2003.10286 (2020)

12. Hochreiter, S., Schmidhuber, J.: Long short-term memory. Neural Comput. **9**(8), 1735–1780 (1997)

13. Jiang, Y., Natarajan, V., Chen, X., Rohrbach, M., Batra, D., Parikh, D.: Pythia v0.1: the winning entry to the VQA challenge 2018. arXiv preprint arXiv:1807.09956 (2018)

14. Kim, J.H., Jun, J., Zhang, B.T.: Bilinear attention networks. In: Advances in Neural Information Processing Systems, vol. 31 (2018)

15. Kovaleva, O., et al.: Towards visual dialog for radiology. In: Proceedings of the 19th SIGBioMed Workshop on Biomedical Language Processing, pp. 60–69 (2020)

16. Lau, J.J., Gayen, S., Ben Abacha, A., Demner-Fushman, D.: A dataset of clinically generated visual questions and answers about radiology images. Sci. Data **5**(1), 1–10 (2018)

17. Lee, J., et al.: BioBERT: a pre-trained biomedical language representation model for biomedical text mining. Bioinformatics **36**(4), 1234–1240 (2020)

18. Nguyen, B.D., Do, T.-T., Nguyen, B.X., Do, T., Tjiputra, E., Tran, Q.D.: Overcoming data limitation in medical visual question answering. In: Shen, D., et al. (eds.) MICCAI 2019. LNCS, vol. 11767, pp. 522–530. Springer, Cham (2019). https://doi.org/10.1007/978-3-030-32251-9_57

19. Pan, H., He, S., Zhang, K., Qu, B., Chen, C., Shi, K.: MuVAM: a multi-view attention-based model for medical visual question answering. arXiv preprint arXiv:2107.03216 (2021)

20. Raghu, M., Zhang, C., Kleinberg, J., Bengio, S.: Transfusion: understanding transfer learning for medical imaging. In: Advances in Neural Information Processing Systems, vol. 32 (2019)

21. Vaswani, A., et al.: Attention is all you need. In: Advances in Neural Information Processing Systems, vol. 30 (2017)

22. Yang, Z., He, X., Gao, J., Deng, L., Smola, A.: Stacked attention networks for image question answering. In: Proceedings of the IEEE Conference on Computer Vision and Pattern Recognition, pp. 21–29 (2016)

23. Zhan, L.M., Liu, B., Fan, L., Chen, J., Wu, X.M.: Medical visual question answering via conditional reasoning. In: Proceedings of the 28th ACM International Conference on Multimedia, pp. 2345–2354 (2020)

24. Zhou, Y., Kang, X., Ren, F.: Employing inception-ResNet-v2 and bi-LSTM for medical domain visual question answering. In: CLEF (Working Notes) (2018)

Deep Robust Neural Networks Inspired by Human Cognitive Bias Against Transfer-based Attacks

Yuuki Ogasawara(✉), Masao Kubo, and Hiroshi Sato(iD)

Department of Computer Science, National Defense Academy of Japan,
Yokosuka, Japan
ogayuukinda@gmail.com, {masaok,hsato}@nda.ac.jp
http://www.nda.ac.jp/~masaok, http://www.nda.ac.jp/~hsato

Abstract. In recent years, with the proliferation of cloud services, the threat of Transfer-based attacks, a type of Adversarial attacks, has increased. Adversarial Training is known as an effective defense against this attack, but it has been pointed out that it degrades accuracy against normal data and robustness against random noise(Gaussian noise). To solve these problems, we focus on the human visual function, which has robustness while maintaining high accuracy. The contribution of top-down processing, in which the feedforward signal is overwritten by some bias factor, has been pointed out as the reason for this. From this perspective, we propose a new model based on Neural Networks using human cognitive bias. This is an algorithm that overwrites signals according to human cognitive bias and is expected to reproduce human visual functions. Evaluation experiments on two different datasets suggest that the proposed model is robust against Transfer-based attacks. Furthermore, the proposed model can mitigate the accuracy degradation of the normal data to a limited extent, suggesting that it is robust against random noise.

Keywords: Adversarial attacks · Adversarial examples · Transfer-based attacks · Random noise · Cognitive bias · Neural networks · Robustness

1 Introduction

Currently, there is a social trend to rely on AI services for critical decision-making, such as translation services, object detection services, authentication systems, and automated driving. Along with this social foundation of AI services, Adversarial attacks [3] that exploit these services are becoming more prevalent. In particular, attacks that aim to degrade the functionality of AI services by creating modified data (Adversarial Examples) as input to Machine Learning (ML) models that lead to incorrect results have become a social problem. Transfer-based attacks [6,15,17] are well-known as one of these attacks, and Adversarial

Y. Kambayashi et al. (Eds.): AICON 2022, LNICST 477, pp. 72–85, 2023.
https://doi.org/10.1007/978-3-031-29126-5_6

Training (AT) [1,12,21] is a defensive method. Transfer-based attacks are attacks in which the attacker creates adversarial examples from predicted models (Surrogate models) and induces misclassification of the ML models, even if the internal information of the ML models are unknown. AT is a method to prevent incorrect results by adding adversarial examples to the ML models training data. Although AT is widely used, it is known to 1) degrade pure service performance (Clean accuracy), and 2) be overly sensitive to random noise [23]. Therefore, it is necessary to develop robust models that can replace AT while suppressing these side effects.

Our goal is to improve "Adversarial robustness" (robustness against Transfer-based attacks) and "Noise robustness" (robustness against random noise) with as little degradation of Clean accuracy as possible. To achieve this goal, we focus on the property that human vision mechanism has Adversarial robustness [7] and Noise robustness [10], while high accuracy rate of about 95% [18]. Computer vision is fully feedforward neural networks and is unidirectional in nature. On the other hand, human vision has feedback functions during feedforward, which means that the signal is overwritten or modified by experience and knowledge. This modification function is believed to reduce the effects of adversarial examples and random noise, allowing for a more essential visual representation [7,10]. Inspired by these findings on vision, we focus on a model called loosely symmetric neural networks (LSNN), which overrides feedforward signals with human cognitive biases. We also developed a new model (LS-DNN), and proposed its application to ML models.

The contributions of this paper are threefold.

(I) LS-DNN has the potential to suppress the range of degradation of Clean accuracy, which is a side effect of Adversarial Training (AT).
(II) It is suggested that LS-DNN has Adversarial robustness.
(III) It is suggested that LS-DNN has Noise robustness.

2 Related Work

2.1 Adversarial Examples

Given adversarial examples x_{adv}, small perturbation $\parallel \delta \parallel_p \in \mathbb{R}^d$, original input $x \in \mathbb{R}^d$, correct label of x $t \in \mathbb{R}^K$, trained parameters θ. We use $f_\theta(x) : \mathbb{R}^d \to \mathbb{R}^K$ to be the ML models function. The prediction class $k(x)$ of x becomes (1).

$$k(x) = \underset{k=1,2,\cdots,K}{\mathrm{argmax}} \ f_{\theta_k}(x) \tag{1}$$

Adversarial examples can be defined by (2) and the task of finding δ to maximize the loss function J, under the constraint that $k(x_{adv}) \neq k(x)$ and $\parallel \delta \parallel_p$ must not be exceeded ε. The optimal $\delta(= \delta^*)$ is given by (3).

$$x_{adv} := x + \delta^* \tag{2}$$

$$\delta^* := \operatorname*{argmax}_{\delta} J(\theta, x_{adv}, t) \quad s.t. \parallel \delta \parallel_p \leq \varepsilon, \ k(x_{adv}) \neq k(x), \ p = \{0, 1, 2, \infty\} \quad (3)$$

Fast Gradient Sign Method (FGSM) and Projected Gradient Descent (PGD) are well known as representative quadrature methods. These are introduced in this paper.

Fast Gradient Sign Method. Goodfellow et al. [12] proposed the Fast Gradient Sign Method (FGSM), which can generate adversarial examples simply and quickly. FGSM computes the sign of the direction in which the loss function $J(\theta, x, t)$ is maximum and adds ε. (see (4)). Here, ε is a hyperparameter that adjusts the magnitude of the perturbation, and the sing function is the function that determines the sign and is (5). Adding this perturbation δ^* to the input x generates adversarial examples x_{adv}.

$$x_{adv} = x + \delta^* = x + \varepsilon \cdot sign(\nabla_x J(\theta, x, t)) \quad (4)$$

$$sign(x) = \begin{cases} 1 & (x > 0) \\ 0 & (x = 0) \\ -1 & (x < 0) \end{cases} \quad (5)$$

Projected Gradient Descent. Madry et al. [1] proposed Projected Gradient Descent (PGD), an improved method of FGSM. This improvement makes it possible to misclassify with fewer perturbations than FGSM since the perturbations are less likely to be noticed by the defender. PGD iteratively updates the perturbation αsmaller than ε every n steps by (6). Where $x + S$ denotes that the norm from the input image is a region within ε.

$$x^{n+1} = \Pi_{x+S}(x^n + \alpha \cdot sign(\nabla_x J(\theta, x^n, t))) \quad (6)$$

2.2   Transfer-Based Attacks

One of the most common attacks using adversarial examples is known as Transfer-based attacks [3, 20] characterized by a property called "Transferability" [6, 17]. Transferability is the property of being affected by adversarial examples between different ML models performing similar tasks. We will refer to the ML models under attack as "Target models" and ML models predicted by the attacker as "Surrogate models". Paternot et al. [16] showed that Target models in the cloud provided by Google and Amazon can be misclassified by Surrogate models. In these cloud services, the internal information of Target models is often unknown, and they only return query results. The attack procedure is described below. 1) The attacker gathers a variety of information in advance. 2) The attacker selects (or creates) and trains Surrogate models based on the gathered information. 3) The attacker creates adversarial examples using learned Surrogate models. 4) The attacker attacks Target models with the adversarial examples to induce misclassification. Thus, Black-box attacks are realistic scenarios, and defensive measures against them are urgent issues. The basic strategy of defensive measures is to construct models with properties that are as immune as possible to the influence of adversarial examples.

2.3 Defense Against Transfer-Based Attacks

The defense methods against Transfer-based attacks can be roughly classified into two categories: attack detection and model robustness. For attack detection, it is pointed out that attack and detection evasion methods are powerful and not sufficiently effective [14]. For the robustness of the model itself, methods that introduce ensembles or use non-differentiable activation functions [4] have been proposed. However, the effects of both of these methods are limited and sufficient robustness has not been achieved.

Adversarial Training (AT). Among the many defense methods, AT is known as the most effective method. Therefore, we use AT as a benchmark against LS-DNN. AT is a method that dynamically generates adversarial examples during training and adds them to the regular data. In other words, the goal is to learn θ to minimize the expected value of the Adversarial error by (7). Where $\mathcal{D}$ denotes the data distribution over which (x, t) pairs exist, $\mathbb{E}$ the expected value, and $\mathcal{S}$ the allowed l_p norm.

$$\min_{\theta}\{\mathbb{E}_{(x,t)\sim\mathcal{D}}[\max_{\delta\in\mathcal{S}} J(\theta, x_{adv}, t)]\} \tag{7}$$

Goodfellow et al. [12] propose a method to introduce a hyperparameter α that adjusts the ratio of adversarial examples by (8).

$$\tilde{J}(\theta, x, t) = \alpha \cdot J(\theta, x_{adv}, t) + (1 - \alpha) \cdot J(\theta, x, t) \tag{8}$$

Problems of Adversarial Training. AT has some problems, and the following 3 negative points are pointed out in this paper. 1) Degrading Clean accuracy. This is because there is a trade-off [11,21] between Adversarial robustness and Clean accuracy. 2) The performance of Adversarial robustness depends on hyperparameters such as Surrogate models architecture [2,20], the algorithm of the adversarial examples [20,21], α in (8). In other words, if the adversarial examples generated by the attacker differs from the hyperparameters used in the AT, the Adversarial robustness performance may be degraded. 3) It is not robust against random noise. Senzaki et al. [23] reported that ML models trained with AT tend to be less accurate against random noise. Random noise is generated by (9) and is evaluated by Random accuracy.

$$x_{rnd} = x + \delta = x + \zeta \cdot sign(\{r_i\}_{i=1...n}) \tag{9}$$

where x_{rnd} is the input with random noise, r_i is a variable following a normal distribution $\mathcal{N}(0, 1)$, n is a variable of x. ζ is a hyperparameter that determines the intensity of the random noise and *sign* function is represented by (5).

3   Proposed Method

3.1   Loosely Symmetric Neural Networks

Taniguchi et al. [9] proposed Loosely Symmetric Neural Networks (LSNN), which is a model of human cognitive bias applied to Neural Networks [5]. LSNN is an attempt to reproduce human physiological causal relationships observed between neurons using the LS model [19]. LSNN architecture consists of three layers: input layer, hidden layer, and output layer, and a logistic sigmoid function is used as the activation function of hidden layer. Now we have Neural Networks with k layers, and the total input to the j node in the k layer (output layer) is x_j^k, and the output of this node is y_j^k. The parameter from the i node in the $k-1$ layer to the j node in the k layer is $\theta_{i,j}^{k-1,k}$. The number of nodes in the $k-1$ layer is n. The output of each node is expressed by (10).

$$x_j^k = \sum_{i=1}^{n} \theta_{i,j}^{k-1,k} \cdot y_i^{k-1} \quad , \qquad y_j^k = \frac{1}{1+e^{-x_j^k}} \tag{10}$$

When the number of nodes in the k layer is m, the loss function J between the output value y_i^k and the true value t_i is MSE, J is expressed by (11). Where δ_i^k is the difference between the network output and the true value.

$$J = \frac{1}{2} \sum_{i=1}^{m} (y_i^k - t_i)^2 = \frac{1}{2} \sum_{i=1}^{m} (\delta_i^k)^2 \tag{11}$$

This loss function J grows in proportion to the square of the difference between the output and true values, Backpropagation is the process of updating the value of the parameter $\theta_{i,j}^{k-1,k}$ so that it decreases. When the learning rate is α, the change in the parameter $\Delta\theta_{i,j}^{k-1,k}$ is calculated by (12).

$$\Delta\theta_{i,j}^{k-1,k} = -\alpha \cdot \delta_j^k \cdot y_j^k(1-y_j^k) \cdot y_i^{k-1} \tag{12}$$

Consider a situation where event p is a cause and event q is a result. Based on the causal relationship between nodes x_j^k and y_i^{k-1}, indicators a, b, c, and d in (Table 1) represent the degree of activity and inactivity of the nodes to which the LS model is applied.

Table 1. Contingency table of the LS model.

p (cause)	q (result)	
	q (x_j^k is activated)	$\neg q$ (x_j^k is not activated)
p (y_i^{k-1} is activated)	$a = y_i^{k-1}$	$b = 1 - y_i^{k-1}$
$\neg p$ (y_i^{k-1} is not activated)	$c = 1 - x_j^k$	$d = x_j^k$

Focusing on the hidden layer node y_i^{k-1} to be overwritten, the conditional probability $P(q|p)$ can be expressed by (13).

$$a = y_i^{k-1} = P(q|p) = \frac{a}{a+b} \tag{13}$$

By adding the bias terms $\frac{bd}{b+d}$ and $\frac{ac}{a+c}$ to the denominator and numerator of $P(q|p)$, LSNN realizes the signal overwriting process in (14).

$$LS(q|p) = LS(y_i^{k-1}) = \frac{a + \frac{bd}{b+d}}{a + b + \frac{ac}{a+c} + \frac{bd}{b+d}} \tag{14}$$

Therefore, the amount of change in the parameters can be expressed by (15).

$$\Delta_{LS}\theta_{i,j}^{k-1,k} = -\alpha \cdot \delta_j^k \cdot y_j^k(1 - y_j^k) \cdot LS(y_i^{k-1}) \tag{15}$$

Thus, the procedure for updating the parameters of the LSNN is as follows, and its architecture is shown in (Fig. 1).

(I) Compute output layer nodes up to the k layer by Feedforward.
(II) Use causality at the k and $k-1$ nodes, and overwrite the value of the $k-1$ node by (14).
(III) Using the values of the hidden layer nodes overwritten by (II), the parameters are updated by Backpropagation.

The procedure (II) is henceforth referred to as the LS Module.

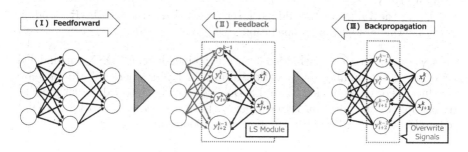

Fig. 1. LSNN architecture.

3.2   LS-DNN Development

We propose LS-DNN (Loosely Symmetric Deep Neural Networks) with additional hidden layers of neural networks and arbitrary number of LS Module applied. The purpose is to determine to what extent the number, position, and combination of LS Module applied to improve robustness and suppress Clean accuracy. In other words, to gain insight into the tendency of cognitive bias to work effectively or counterproductively. In this paper, we have created a simple all-coupled DNN model with up to 5 layers ($k = 5$). Thus, the procedure for updating the parameters of the LS-DNN is as follows, and its architecture is shown in (Fig. 2).

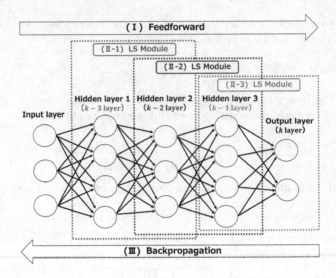

Fig. 2. LS-DNN architecture.

(I) Feedforward computes the output of nodes up to the k layer (output layer).

(II) Select any hidden layer ($k - 3$, $k - 2$, $k - 1$) and overwrite the values of all hidden nodes by the LS Module, starting from the hidden layer closest to the input layer.

(III) Using the values of the hidden layer nodes overwritten with (II), update the parameters by Backpropagation.

The selection of an arbitrary hidden layer is explained here. LS-DNN are modeled according to the number and location of hidden layers where LS Modules are introduced. For example, for $k = 5$, LS-DNN is classified into 7 different models. An example of the notation is given below. LS(12) represents two LS Modules (red and blue dotted boxes) in the first and second hidden layers.

4   Experiments and Discussion

4.1   Methods

Evaluation experiments are based on Papernot et al.'s proposed method [16]. Experimental scenarios assume that an accurate dataset has already been obtained through prior information gathering, but information on the Target models are unknown. We used MNIST dataset [22] and Fashion-MNIST dataset [8]. These are well-known datasets for 10-class classification tasks. 60,000 training data and 10,000 test data are pre-populated with the correct answers labeled. The computer server used in the experiments is Ubuntu 20.04 OS, Intel(R) Xeon(R) CPU E5-2690 v4 @ 2.60GH, and 503GB memory. LS-DNN is evaluated in three experiments. 1) Accuracy against normal data(Clean accuracy) and Training time. 2) Accuracy against adversarial examples(Adversarial accuracy). 3) Accuracy against random noise(Random accuracy). As for 1), LS-DNN is expected to be computationally expensive due to feedback structure. For service providers, the additional computation time for training is a cost to develop and maintain. Therefore, we also evaluate the training time. (Fig. 3) shows images of the 1st experiment(Exp-1), the 2nd experiment(Exp-2), and the 3rd experiment(Exp-3).

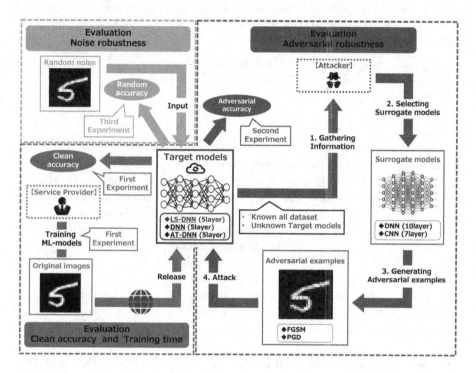

Fig. 3. Image of the Experiments (1st Experiment, 2nd Experiment, 3rd Experiment).

The purpose of the Exp-1 is to verify whether the reduction in Clean accuracy was suppressed and to measure the training time. The evaluation method of Clean accuracy is the accuracy of the Target models against 10,000 pieces of normal test data. The evaluation method of training time is the total CPU execution time from the start to the end of training on 60,000 training data. The purpose of the Exp-2 is to verify whether Adversarial robustness has been obtained. The evaluation method is the Adversarial accuracy of the Target models on 10,000 pieces of adversarial examples. We generate adversarial examples by FGSM and PGD using 10,000 normal all test data. Adversarial accuracy is then verified by continuously increasing the hyperparameter ε. The purpose of the Exp-3 is to verify whether Noise robustness has been obtained. The evaluation method is the Random accuracy of Target models against 10,000 pieces of random noise. We generate random noise by (9) using 10,000 normal all test data. Random accuracy is then verified by continuously increasing the hyperparameter ζ.

4.2 Conditions

Adversarial examples are generated by using framework Adversarial robustness Toolbox (ART) [13]. Target and Surrogate models architectures are shown in (Table 2).

Table 2. Surrogate and Target models architectures used in the experiments. Each layer indicates the type of connection and the magnitude of the output. For the CNN, the padding is set to 0, the stride is set to 1, the filter size to 3×3, and the number of filters are 32 and 64.

	Target models	Surrogate models	
		DNN	CNN
Model Type	LS-DNN DNN AT-DNN	DNN	CNN
Layers	5	10	7
Input	Flatten(784)	Flatten(784)	28×28
hidden	Fully Connected(50)	Fully Connected(100)	Convolution (26×26×32)
	Fully Connected(50)	Fully Connected(100)	MaxPooling(13×13×32)
	Fully Connected(50)	Fully Connected(100)	Convolution (11×11×64)
	–	Fully Connected(100)	MaxPooling(5×5×64)
	–	Fully Connected(100)	Fully Connected(1600)
	–	Fully Connected(100)	–
	–	Fully Connected(100)	–
	–	Fully Connected(100)	–
Output	Fully Connected(10)	Fully Connected(10)	Fully Connected(10)
Activation	Sigmoid and Softmax	Sigmoid and Softmax	ReLU and Softmax

Target models architectures are three different models (LS-DNN, DNN, and AT-DNN), and their performance is compared. Surrogate models architectures are DNN and CNN. This is to verify whether the Adversarial robustness performance of the LS-DNN depends on Surrogate models architecture. We explain why we changed the number of hidden layers in the DNN of the Target and Surrogate models. The more similar Target and Surrogate models architectures are, the more susceptible they are to transferability [15] and the more difficult it is to verify accurate Adversarial robustness. For Target and Surrogate models, we set learning rate = 0.001, optimizer = RMSProp, epoch = 100, and minibatch = 50. Adversarial examples were generated continuously with ε ranging from 0.0 $\sim$ 0.3 in 0.05 increments. For PGD, $\alpha = 0.01$ and $n = 40$ in (6). AT-DNN is based on the previous study [1,12]. FGSM is set to $\varepsilon = 0.25$, PGD is set to $\varepsilon = 0.3$ and $\alpha = 0.01$. We trained different models with the ratio adjustment hyperparameter $\alpha = 0.1, 0.5, 0.9$ in (8). All other hyperparameters were set to the ART default values.

4.3   Results

The results of Exp-1 are shown in (Table 3). Supplemental information about AT-DNN. We created six patterns of AT-DNN by using two different adversarial examples generation methods (FGSM and PGD) and three different $\alpha = 0.1, 0.5, 0.9$ in (8). For example, AT(FGSM(0.1)) is an AT-DNN that generates adversarial examples by FGSM and AT with $\alpha = 0.1$.

Table 3. Clean accuracy(Train(%) and Test(%)) and training time(Time(s)) against MNIST and Fashion-MNIST dataset of Target models: LS-DNN(Proposed method), DNN(Original), AT-DNN(Comparative method).

Target models		MNIST			Fashion-MNIST		
		Train(%)	Test(%)	Time(s)	Train(%)	Test(%)	Time(s)
LS-DNN (Proposed-method)	LS(1)	97.49	95.51	41,431	89.35	86.24	40,403
	LS(2)	98.02	95.74	41,518	89.83	86.74	41,362
	LS(3)	97.71	95.84	16,746	89.87	86.71	15,523
	LS(12)	93.66	92.87	71,493	87.84	85.31	72,408
	LS(13)	96.54	95.24	47,685	88.99	86.01	47,133
	LS(23)	96.41	95.28	47,745	88.33	85.59	49,988
	LS(123)	92.99	92.41	77,884	84.74	83.12	78,936
DNN (Original)	DNN	98.51	95.99	1,192	90.27	86.39	1,417
AT-DNN (Comparative-method)	AT(FGSM(0.1))	99.41	97.10	1,569	94.45	87.55	1,241
	AT(FGSM(0.5))	96.34	95.60	1,677	89.86	86.43	1,393
	AT(FGSM(0.9))	89.03	89.40	2,151	82.29	81.19	1,718
	AT(PGD(0.1))	99.17	97.73	11,031	92.24	87.72	12,610
	AT(PGD(0.5))	94.40	94.41	15,384	82.81	81.74	14,705
	AT(PGD(0.9))	82.83	82.70	28,407	65.73	65.44	27,935

First, we will discuss Clean accuracy and training time in Exp-1. As for Clean accuracy, LS-DNN showed locally higher values than AT-DNN. In particular, for all LS-DNN, the values were higher than those of the AT(FGSM(0.9)) and AT(PGD(0.9)). However, LS-DNN tends to degrade when the number of LS Module is increased. This can be interpreted as overdone signal overwrite modification promoting degrade Clean accuracy. As for training time, compared to AT-DNN and DNN models, the training time increased significantly. The increase in computational complexity as the number of LS mechanisms increases can be attributed to the feedback function of the LS-DNN.

The results of Exp-2 are shown in (Fig. 4) $\sim$ (Fig. 7). It plots the change in the corresponding Adversarial accuracy when ε is increased by 0.05 from $0 \sim 0.3$ in FGSM and PGD. MNIST dataset shows in (Fig. 4) and (Fig. 5). Fashion-MNIST dataset shows in (Fig. 6) and (Fig. 7).

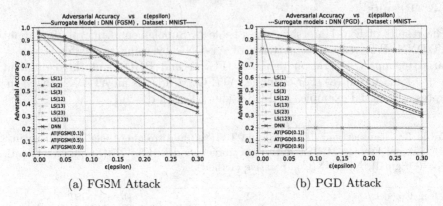

(a) FGSM Attack

(b) PGD Attack

Fig. 4. Adversarial accuracy against MNIST (Surrogate models: DNN).

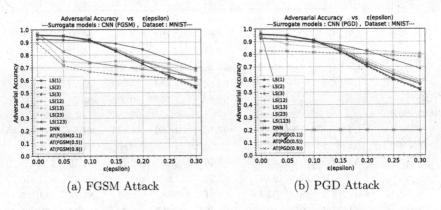

(a) FGSM Attack

(b) PGD Attack

Fig. 5. Adversarial accuracy against MNIST (Surrogate models: CNN).

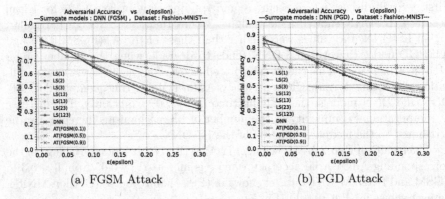

(a) FGSM Attack

(b) PGD Attack

Fig. 6. Adversarial accuracy against Fashion-MNIST (Surrogate models: DNN).

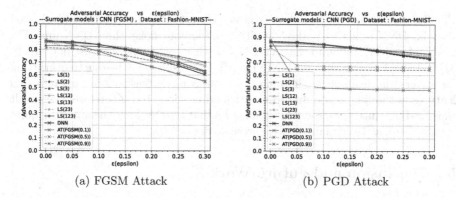

(a) FGSM Attack   (b) PGD Attack

Fig. 7. Adversarial accuracy against Fashion-MNIST (Surrogate models: CNN).

Next, we will discuss two perspectives on Adversarial robustness in Exp-2. The first focus is on the number of times the LS Module is applied. We found that increasing the number of times the LS Module is applied tends to improve Adversarial robustness. Furthermore, this trend is independent of the dataset and Surrogate models architecture. It can be assumed that the more often an architecture processes signal overwriting, the more parameters are changed, and thus the gradient similarity with the Surrogate models can be relatively small [2]. The second focus is on the difference in Surrogate models architecture. When the Surrogate models is DNN, LS-DNN has weaker Adversarial robustness than AT-DNN, but stronger than DNN. On the other hand, when the Surrogate models is CNN, AT-DNN has weaker Adversarial robustness than both LS-DNN and DNN. These results were observed regardless of the type of dataset used. This suggests that LS-DNN have more generalized Adversarial robustness independent of Surrogate models architecture.

The results of Exp-3 are shown in (Fig. 8). This plots the change in the corresponding Random accuracy when ζ is increased by 0.05 from $0 \sim 0.3$. Note that the random noise is clipped between $[0, 1]$ to adjust the output.

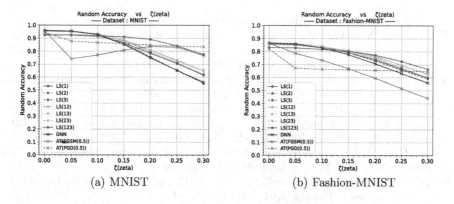

(a) MNIST   (b) Fashion-MNIST

Fig. 8. Random accuracy against MNIST and Fashion-MNIST.

Finally, we will discuss Noise robustness in Exp-3. Experimental results showed that LS-DNN tends to be less sensitive to random noise than DNN and AT-DNN. Moreover, we found that AT-DNN is sensitive to random noise not only in MNIST [23] but also Fashion-MNIST [8]. Those results may be due to overfitting for adversarial examples. The reason for the Noise robustness of human visual features is thought to be due to signal modification [10]. Therefore, the result that LS-DNN has Noise robustness suggests that LS-DNN may be able to acquire features similar to human visual representations.

5   Conclusion and Future Work

In this paper, we proposed to apply LS-DNN to Target models against Transfer-based attacks. The results showed that LS-DNN has Adversarial robustness independent of the Surrogate models architecture. We also showed that LS-DNN can overcome the problems of the AT, such as "degrade Clean accuracy" and "be overly sensitive to random noise."

Three issues for the future are listed below. The first is theoretical analysis. As Demontis et al. [2] point out, it is necessary to calculate the gradient alignment of the loss functions of LS-DNN and Surrogate models, and clarify their correlation. The second is the mitigation of "degrade Clean accuracy." We found that LS-DNN has a trade-off relationship between Adversarial robustness and Clean accuracy. Therefore, it is expected to optimize the number and placement of the LS Module. The third is reduction of the computation time for training. Compared to DNN and AT-DNN, LS-DNN is computationally more expensive due to its architecture. In parallel, we plan to investigate methods using the LS Module against attacks other than Transfer-based attacks.

References

1. Madry, A., Makelov, A., Schmidt, L., et al.: Towards deep learning models resistant to adversarial attacks. In: 6th International Conference on Learning Representations, ICLR 2018, Vancouver, BC, Canada, 30 April - 3 May 2018, Conference Track Proceedings. OpenReview.net (2018)
2. Demontis, A., Melis, M., Pintor, M., et al.: Why do adversarial attacks transfer? Explaining transferability of evasion and poisoning attacks. In: 28th USENIX security symposium (USENIX security 19), pp. 321–338 (2019)
3. Chakraborty, A., Alam, M., Dey, V., et al.: A survey on adversarial attacks and defences. CAAI Trans. Intell. Technol. **6**(1), 25–45 (2021)
4. Xiao, C., Zhong, P., Zheng, C.: Enhancing adversarial defense by k-winners-take-all. In: 8th International Conference on Learning Representations. ICLR 2020, Addis Ababa, Ethiopia, 26–30 April 2020. OpenReview.net (2020)
5. Rumelhart, D.E., Hinton, G.E., Williams, R.J.: Learning representations by back-propagating errors. Nature **323**(6088), 533–536 (1986)
6. Tramèr, F., Papernot, N., Goodfellow, I.J., et al.: The space of transferable adversarial examples. CoRR abs/1704.03453 (2017)

7. Elsayed, F.G., Shankar, S., Cheung, B., et al.: Adversarial examples that fool both computer vision and time-limited humans. In: Advances in Neural Information Processing Systems, vol. 31 (2018)
8. Xiao, H., Rasul, K., Vollgraf, R.: Fashion-mnist: a novel image dataset for bench-marking machine learning algorithms. arXiv:1708.07747 (2017)
9. Taniguchi, H., Sato, H., Shirakawa, T.: Implementation of human cognitive bias on neural network and its application to breast cancer diagnosis. SICE J. Control Meas. Syst. Integr. **12**(2), 56–64 (2019)
10. Jang, H., McCormack, D., Tong, F.: Noise-robust recognition of objects by humans and deep neural networks. bioRxiv, pp. 2020–08 (2021)
11. Zhang, H., Yu, Y., Jiao, J., et al.: Theoretically principled trade-off between robust-ness and accuracy. In: International Conference on Machine Learning, pp. 7472–7482. PMLR (2019)
12. Goodfellow, I.J., Shlens, J., Szegedy, C.: Explaining and harnessing adversarial examples. In: Bengio, Y.Y.L. (ed.) 3rd International Conference on Learning Rep-resentations, ICLR 2015, San Diego, CA, USA, 7–9 May 2015, Conference Track Proceedings (2015)
13. Nicolae, M.-I., Sinn, M., Tran, M.N., et al.: Adversarial robustness toolbox v0.2.2. CoRR abs/1807.01069 (2018)
14. Carlini, N., Wagner, D.A.: Towards evaluating the robustness of neural networks. In: 2017 IEEE Symposium on Security and Privacy (S&P), pp. 39–57. IEEE (2017)
15. Papernot, N., McDaniel, P., Goodfellow, I.J.: Transferability in machine learn-ing: from phenomena to black-box attacks using adversarial samples. CoRR abs/1605.07277 (2016)
16. Papernot, N., McDaniel, P.D., Goodfellow, I., et al.: Practical black-box attacks against machine learning. In: Proceedings of the 2017 ACM on Asia Conference on Computer and Communications Security, pp. 506–519 (2017)
17. Papernot, N., McDaniel, P.D., Jha, S., et al.: The limitations of deep learning in adversarial settings. In: 2016 IEEE European Symposium on Security and Privacy (EuroS&P), pp. 372–387. IEEE (2016)
18. Russakovsky, O., Deng, J., Hao, S., et al.: ImageNet large scale visual recognition challenge. Int. J. Comput. Vis. **115**(3), 211–252 (2015). https://doi.org/10.1007/s11263-015-0816-y
19. Shinohara, S., Taguchi, R., Katsurada, K., et al.: A model of belief formation based on causality and application to n-armed bandit problem. Trans. Japan. Soc. Artif. Intell. **22**(1), 58–68 (2007)
20. Bhambri, S., Muku, S., Tulasi, A., et al.: A study of black box adversarial attacks in computer vision. CoRR abs/1912.01667 (2019)
21. Bai, T., Luo, J., Zhao, J., et al.: Recent advances in adversarial training for adver-sarial robustness. In: Zhou, Z. (ed.) Proceedings of the Thirtieth International Joint Conference on Artificial Intelligence, IJCAI 2021, Virtual Event / Montreal, Canada, 19–27 August 2021, pp. 4312–4321. ijcai.org (2021)
22. LeCun, Y., Cortes, C., Burges, C.J.C.: MNIST handwritten digit database. http://yann.lecun.com/exdb/mnist/. Accessed 15 June 2022
23. Senzaki, Y., Ohata, S., Matsuura, K.: Negative side effect of adversarial training in deep learning and its mitigation. In: 2017 Information Processing Society of Japan, vol. 2017(2) (2017)

Efficient Estimation of Cow's Location Using Machine Learning Based on Sensor Data

Tomohide Sawada[✉], Tom Uchino, Niken P. Martono, and Hayato Ohwada

Department of Industrial Administration, Faculty of Science and Technology,
Tokyo University of Science, Tokyo, Japan
{7422519,7421701}@ed.tus.ac.jp, {niken,ohwada}@rs.tus.ac.jp

Abstract. Indoor localization of dairy cows is important for determining cow behavior and enabling an effective farm management. In this study, a low-cost localization system was constructed by attaching accelerometers to dairy cows kept indoors in a barn in order to obtain radio wave strength. Using link quality indicator (LQI) data, we employed four machine learning models to predict the position of the cow: LightGBM, logistic regression, support vector machine (SVM), and neural network. The prediction performance and computational cost of the models were compared and evaluated. In the monitoring and building of the prediction models for cow's location, we considered various sizes of location (barn) compartments and evaluated the performance of each prediction model using with different compartments. The experimental results showed that LightGBM and neural networks have an accuracy of 46.6% at 9 m horizontal and 12 m vertical and an accuracy of 90% at 45 m horizontal and 15 m vertical. In terms of the computational score, we may consider whether to use neural network or LightGBM depending on the amount of data to be predicted at a time in the location estimation system.

Keywords: Indoor localization · Machine learning · Sensor data · Farm management · Cow location

1 Introduction

In Japan, almost all dairy cows are housed indoors at least for some part of their lives, and, in an increasing number of farms, indoor housing is practiced year-round. Farmers are preferring to keep their cows indoors throughout the year [8] since it allows them to provide high-yielding individuals with a nutritionally balanced diet fit for their needs, and this practice has important welfare benefits for both cows and their calves, such as protection from predators, parasites, and exposure to extreme weather conditions. However, the challenge is that farmers need to visually check the location of each cow, as there are typically more than 100 cows in a barn.

© ICST Institute for Computer Sciences, Social Informatics and Telecommunications Engineering 2023
Published by Springer Nature Switzerland AG 2023. All Rights Reserved
Y. Kambayashi et al. (Eds.): AICON 2022, LNICST 477, pp. 86–94, 2023.
https://doi.org/10.1007/978-3-031-29126-5_7

The motions and location of animals are important for their health monitoring. By monitoring the motions of animals, we may obtain early warnings of diseases and stresses by analyzing untypical behavior. Several commercial systems that can monitor cow behavior have been based on cow motions. However, these systems are relatively expensive [4]. Many studies have been conducted on the position estimation of indoor cows using the received signal strength indicator(RSSI) values, which can be obtained from Wifi access points (APs) and link quality indication (LQI), which can be obtained from ZigBee modules based on the IEEE 802.15.4 standard. There are several methods for indoor location estimation using radio wave strength, such as trilateration [11] and the fingerprint method, which can predict data most similar to past data.

In this study, we constructed a mechanical localization system by attaching accelerometers that can acquire radio wave strength to dairy cows kept indoors in a barn. The proposed system can support dairy farmers to visually estimating the position of their cows by illuminating the LEDs on the accelerometers and displaying their location on a web application, thereby assisting in quick response to sick cows and in health management tasks. We trained a machine learning model with pairs of radio wave strength and location labels obtained from multiple APs to create a model that can predict the location using radio wave strength data from multiple APs. Four machine learning algorithms were considered for position estimation: LightGBM, logistic regression, support vector machine (SVM), and neural network. The results were compared and evaluated both accuracy and computational cost. Finally, we considered various sizes of the predicted location compartments for actual operation of the location estimation system for dairy cows kept in a free stall barn and evaluated each model for each compartment size.

2 Related Works

There is growing interest in developing technologies that can help monitor the physiological and behavioral parameters of dairy cows [5], mainly attributed to the increase in herd size and the facilitation of herd and health management. A good dairy management system should include automated milking systems and automated feeders as well as sensors (e.g., pedometers and accelerometers) that can be mounted on a cow's legs, collars, or ears or placed in the rumen. Additionally, it should include real-time location systems that allow tracking of animal location within a barn.

These systems can be useful for detecting cows within the barn, for example, in estimating and predicting the time animals spend in relevant areas, such as the alley, feed bunk, or cubicle [5]. Location data can also be used to predict the activity performed by animals in important areas of the barn. Many indoor location estimation methods for cows have been studied and reviewed. In particular, location estimation using machine learning models has been extensively studied.

RADAR is a pioneering RF-based fingerprint indoor location estimation method that uses the K-nearest neighbour (KNN) and Euclidean distance as the location estimation index between the predicted and actual locations [3]. Previous studies have also introduced machine learning models, such as the support vector machine (SVM) [6,9], random forest (RF) [7], decision tree [10], and deep learning models to address the inherent problems in indoor positioning, showing good performance in analyzing the indoor positioning of animals. Various machine learning algorithms, such as deep learning, have been used for location estimation using RSSI values, and methods using it [1,2] have been devised. However, there have been few stduies on location estimation using LQI data. Moreover, the accuracy of these multiple algorithms and the computational cost of actually operating them have not been compared. Our work addresses these gaps. We employed LQI data from sensors and used several machine learning algorithms to create location prediction model for cows, and their performance was compared and evaluated.

3   Methods

3.1   Data Acquisition

The LQI data used in this study were obtained from accelerometers attached to approximately 100 Holstein dairy cows at Nakayama Farm in Nakashibetsu, Hokkaido, Japan. The period of data acquisition was from April 29 to 30, 2021, and the total number of data points was 126,696. The data range was a closed interval from 0 to 255. We used 70% of the total data by random sampling in the training sample, and 30% for the test sample. Some of the missing values were preprocessed before being used in the model building. In the barn where the data were obtained, a fixed transponder was installed to acquire the radio wave from the accelerometer, as shown in Fig. 1. The barn was 19.4 m long and 78.8 m wide, with a 5.4 m-wide aisle at the center. The actual length and width of each compartment where the dairy cows were kept was 12 m as seen from the entrance of the barn. In this study, the barn was divided into 160 sections, 80 sections on each side viewed from the barn entrance, and approximately 790 data were obtained from each section. The length and width of each section of the 160 compartments were 3 m and 3.94 m, respectively.

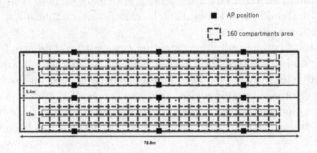

Fig. 1. Barn layout and AP position

The LQI value is the link evaluation value based on the bit error rate (BER), which is the loss rate of packets with a value between 0 and 255. The accelerometer used for acquiring the LQI values was attached around the neck of the dairy cow. For efficiency reasons, we set a separate accelerometer that can transmit acceleration data to a fixed relay once every 0.25 s for data acquisition.

At Nakayama Farm, where the data were obtained, the reception of acceleration data from the radio waves emitted by the accelerometer and the acquisition of LQI values were performed using a fixed repeater, as shown in Fig. 1. The repeater used in the experiment was a Raspberry Pi Zero WH connected to a 32-bit wireless microcontroller module TWELITE DIP (developed by Mono Wireless) that complies with IEEE802.15.4. After the fixed transponder sends the acceleration data from the accelerometers via Zigbee communication, the data were sent to the server. A server was installed at each barn, and Raspberry Pi 4 model B was used as the hardware. The servers measured the computational cost (the time cost of making predictions using the trained models), which was used to compare the accuracy of each machine learning model as well as their computational cost.

3.2 Data Preprocessing

As a preprocessing step for the completion of missing values, we set the LQI value to -1 when the transponder could not acquire a signal, i.e., when the LQI value could not be acquired. This is because the value range of the data includes 0, and -1 is used to distinguish them from the data whose values are close to 0, although they can be acquired by the transponders. To examine the grouping of the divisions, we divided the barn into two regions: the left and right sides from the barn entrance. We divided the barn vertically into two compartments (each 78.8 m in length and 12 m in width), 8 compartments (each 19.7 m in length and 12 m in width), and 20 compartments (each 15.76 m in length and 6 m in width), respectively, as shown in Figs. 2, 3 and 4.

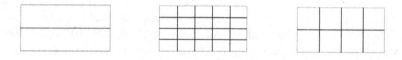

Fig. 2. 2 partitions   **Fig. 3.** 8 partitions   **Fig. 4.** 20 partitions

3.3 Machine Learning Model

In this study, Bayesian optimization was applied to decide the hyperparameter values of each method using Optuna to improve the performance of each model. The trained models with the hyperparameters optimized by Optuna were also used to determine the computational cost of the operation. In using the machine learning, the main purpose is to learn to minimize the cross-entropy error.

Equation 1 shows the dateset in building the machine learning model: the dataset is denoted by $\boldsymbol{D}$, the feature LQI value is $\boldsymbol{x}$, the area of the teacher data is $\boldsymbol{A}$, the number of parts is $\boldsymbol{d}$ ($\boldsymbol{d} \in \{2, 8, 20, 160\}, \boldsymbol{A} \in \{A_1, A_2, \ldots, A_d\}$) and the amount of data is M ($M = 126, 969$).

$$D = \begin{pmatrix} LQI_{1,AP1} & \cdots & LQI_{1,APj} & \cdots & LQI_{1,AP12} \\ \vdots & & \vdots & & \vdots \\ LQI_{i,AP1} & \cdots & LQI_{i,APj} & \cdots & LQI_{i,AP12} \\ \vdots & & \vdots & & \vdots \\ LQI_{M,AP1} & \cdots & LQI_{M,APj} & \cdots & LQI_{M,AP12} \end{pmatrix} \tag{1}$$

$$\boldsymbol{D} \in \mathbb{R}^{M,12}, \boldsymbol{x} \in \boldsymbol{D}, \boldsymbol{A} \in \mathbb{R}^d.$$

Given the LQI value $\boldsymbol{x}$ of a certain target acquired by each relay from the data, considering the posterior probability $\boldsymbol{P}(A_j|\boldsymbol{x})$ that the target is in an area A_j, and finding its likelihood, the model parameters are $\boldsymbol{\theta}$, the likelihood function is $\boldsymbol{P} = \boldsymbol{P}(\boldsymbol{A}|\boldsymbol{x})$, and $\boldsymbol{t}$ is a one-hot matrix of the teacher data. The likelihood function is obtained as follows:

$$L(\boldsymbol{\theta}) = \prod_{i=1}^{M} \prod_{j=1}^{d} p_{ij}{}^{t_{ij}} \tag{2}$$

We minimize the logarithm of the likelihood function $L(\boldsymbol{\theta})$ using a machine learning model to minimize the cross-entropy: $-ln(L(\boldsymbol{\theta}))$. To evaluate the learning model, the percentage of correct predictions is calculated for each of the three partitions considered for each learner: 2 partitions, 8 partitions, 20 partitions, and 160 partitions. For the 20-part and 160-part partitioning methods, a percentage of correctness is also evaluated by assuming that when one part is predicted, it is said to be correct if its neighboring part has the correct label.

For all the partitioning methods, 70% of the data randomly sampled from the entire dataset was used as training data and the other 30% was used as test data. The evaluation index for each trainer was also set to be the usual percentage of correct predictions. For the evaluation of the computational complexity, we measured the time required to make predictions on 1,000, 100, 10, and 1 data points for each of the partitioning methods considered by each trainer using a Raspberry Pi 4 model B.

Prediction models were build using four machine learning algorithms:

- **Logistic regression (LR).** LR is a simple but powerful algorithm for linear classification regression problems, binary classification problems, and multiclass classification; it is a model for classification rather than regression. In this study, given a feature $\boldsymbol{x}$, we performed a multiclass classification to determine whether the target belongs to area A_i or not.
- **LightGBM.** The light gradient boosing machine(LightGBM) is a type of gradient boosting that uses the gradient descent method to minimize the loss function when constructing a weak learner among boosting methods that

sequentially construct weak learners and generate prediction models. The tree structure is such that the tree is grown leaf by leaf and the leaf with the lowest loss is selected, which has the advantage of high efficiency and memory consumption.

- **Support vector machines (SVM).** The SVM is one of the widely used and powerful algorithms that maximizes the margin between the hyperplane (decision boundary), which is the decision boundary to classify positive or negative cases, and the training sample closest to the hyperplane.
- **Neural network (NN).** A neural network comprises an input layer, an intermediate layer, and an output layer. It learns by gradually adjusting the weights of each layer to reduce the error between the correct label and the correct answer. In this study, we used TensorFlow to construct and train a neural network with the structure shown in Fig. 5.

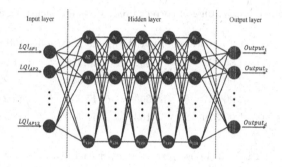

Fig. 5. Structure of the neural network model

4   Results and Discussion

Table 1 presents the accuracy of each of the segmentation methods used in the experiment, namely logistic regression, SVM, LightGBM, and neural network, for the 160-, 20-, 8-, and 2-part segmentations. Table 2 presents the loose accuracy rates for the 160-part and 20-part partitions, where the parts adjacent to the predicted part are also considered as correct. For the 160-part split, the results in Table 1 show that LightGBM has the highest percentage of correct predictions. In addition, Table 2 shows that LightGBM and the neural network have the highest percentage of loose correct predictions, and their numbers are almost similar. The accuracy of guessing the correct answer for each segment is less than 20% for all the training systems; however, when the loose accuracy, which is the percentage of correct predictions for segments adjacent to each segment, is used as an indicator, all the training systems achieve an accuracy rate higher than 40%, and the accuracy rate of LightGBM and neural network is close to 50%.

The results show that the accuracy, is 46.6% at 9 m (width) and 12 m (height). Using the 20 part splits, the highest percentage of correct predictions is obtained for LightGBM when looking at the results presented in Table 1. Moreover, from Table 2, the SVM has the highest percentage of loose correct predictions. The LightGBM and neural network are almost as accurate as the SVM. As for the accuracy of guessing each compartment, models other than logistic regression have an accuracy close to 50%, and above 90% for the loose correct rate. From these results, it can be said that an accuracy of 90% is achieved at 45 m (width) and 18 m (height).

Using the 8-partition classification, Table 1 shows that LightGBM has the highest percentage of correct predictions. The neural network and LightGBM have largely the same accuracy, being close to 60%. Finally, for the two-partition classification, Table 1 shows that LightGBM has the highest accuracy rate, and all the models except for logistic regression have an accuracy of more than 90%, with no significant difference in the accuracies between the SVM, neural network, and LightGBM.

Table 1. Percentage of correct predictions for each learner

ML model	2 partitions	8 partitions	20 partitions	160 partitions
Logistic regression	85.927	51.006	40.459	11.966
SVM	90.247	56.987	47.649	18.222
LightGBM	90.657	58.660	47.907	19.217
Neural network	90.379	58.163	47.147	18.183

Table 2. Loose correct rate for each learner

ML model	20 partitions	160 partitions
Logistic regression	89.979	40.990
SVM	91.360	44.679
LightGBM	91.344	46.694
Neural network	91.242	46.699

Table 3 shows the time required by the logistic regression, SVM, LightGBM and neural network segmentation methods to predict 1,000, 100, 10, and 1 data point(s) for 160 partitions, 20 partitions, 8 partitions, and 2 partitions. For the 160-part and 20-part partitions, in terms of the forecasting time required by LightGBM and neural network, which have a high forecasting accuracy, Light-GBM is faster than the neural network except for forecasting 1,000 cases. Light-GBM is faster than the neural network in predicting 1 to 100 data points. For the 8-part classification and 2-part segmentation, LightGBM, which is the best in terms of accuracy, is the fastest in all cases, except for the 160-part segmentation and 20-part segmentation. In the case of 160-part or 20-part segmentation, where more than 1,000 predictions are required in actual operation, it is necessary to select a trainer that can balance the ideal accuracy and computational cost between the neural network and LightGBM.

Table 3. Computational cost of predicting each classifier

ML model	Number of part divisions	1,000 case [msec]	100 case [msec]	10 case [msec]	1 case [msec]
Logistic regression	160	273	281	285	289
	20	46.7	50.9	54.9	58.7
	8	29.1	33.3	37.4	41.4
	2	14.7	19.2	23.5	27.9
SVM	160	8.88×10^4	8.94×10^3	903	106
	20	2.30×10^4	2.29×10^3	242	29.7
	8	1.86×10^4	1.87×10^3	189	24.9
	2	1.63×10^4	1.64×10^3	173	23.1
LightGBM	160	1.89×10^3	176	25.1	11.1
	20	290	33.3	8.38	6.01
	8	19.3	6.43	6.13	4.91
	2	19.3	6.43	5.12	4.91
Neural network	160	254	134	124	123
	20	230	133	126	123
	8	238	133	126	123
	2	236	134	124	122

5 Conclusions

This study developed a method for estimating the location of individual dairy cows indoors using a machine learning model and LQI values as the radio wave strength for the dataset. Four machine learning models, namely logistic regression, SVM, LightGBM, and neural network, were employed to build prediction models. As an evaluation of the accuracy of the models, we examined the percentage of correct predictions and the percentage of loose predictions in which a predicted segment is also considered to be correct if it is adjacent to the predicted segment. We also examined the prediction time required by each model on a real machine and compared the computational cost of operating the system to verify the best model for operating a location estimation system. Finally, we examined 160-part, 20-part, 8-part, and 2-part partitions as the classification partitions.

The proposed method could make loose correct predictions with an accuracy of 90% for the 20-part classification and 2-part classification and with accuracies of 46% and 56% for the 160-part and 8-part divisions, respectively. In terms of the computational complexity, it is necessary to consider whether to use the neural network or LightGBM for the 160-part or 20-part segmentation, depending on the amount of data to be predicted at a time in the location estimation system. In the future, for barns where dairy cows are kept, we plan to analyze the variation in the LQI due to environmental factors such as humidity and temperature, and consider improving the accuracy by adding environmental information as a new feature.

References

1. Abdull Sukor, A.S., Kamarudin, L.M., Zakaria, A., Abdul Rahim, N., Sudin, S., Nishizaki, H.: RSSI-based for device-free localization using deep learning technique. Smart Cities 3(2), 444–455 (2020). https://doi.org/10.3390/smartcities3020024
2. Ahmadi, H., Bouallegue, R.: Exploiting machine learning strategies and RSSI for localization in wireless sensor networks: a survey. In: 2017 13th International Wireless Communications and Mobile Computing Conference (IWCMC), pp. 1150–1154 (2017). https://doi.org/10.1109/IWCMC.2017.7986447
3. Bahl, P., Padmanabhan, V.: RADAR: an in-building RF-based user location and tracking system. In: Proceedings IEEE INFOCOM 2000, vol. 2, pp. 775–784 (2000). https://doi.org/10.1109/INFCOM.2000.832252
4. Bloch, V., Pastell, M.: Monitoring of cow location in a barn by an opensource, low-cost, low-energy bluetooth tag system. Sensors 20(14), 3841 (2020). https://doi.org/10.3390/s20143841
5. Chapa, J.M., et al.: Use of a real-time location system to detect cows in distinct functional areas within a barn. JDS Commun. 2(4), 217–222 (2021)
6. Chriki, A., Touati, H., Snoussi, H.: SVM-based indoor localization in wireless sensor networks. In: 2017 13th International Wireless Communications and Mobile Computing Conference (IWCMC), pp. 1144–1149 (2017)
7. Guo, X., Ansari, N., Li, L., Li, H.: Indoor localization by fusing a group of fingerprints based on random forests. IEEE Internet Things J. 5(6), 4686–4698 (2017)
8. Mandel, R., Whay, H.R., Klement, E., Nicol, C.J.: Invited review: environmental enrichment of dairy cows and calves in indoor housing. J. Dairy Sci. 99, 1695–1715 (2016). https://doi.org/10.3168/jds.2015-9875
9. Sallouha, H., Chiumento, A., Pollin, S.: Localization in long-range ultra narrow band IoT networks using RSSI. In: 2017 IEEE International Conference on Communications (ICC), pp. 1–6. IEEE (2017). https://doi.org/10.1109/ICC.2017.7997195
10. Sanchez-Rodriguez, D., Hernández-Morera, P., Quinteiro, J., Alonso-González, I.: A low complexity system based on multiple weighted decision trees for indoor localization. Sensors 15, 14809–14829 (2015). https://doi.org/10.3390/s150614809
11. Zhang, D., Xia, F., Yang, Z., Yao, L., Zhao, W.: Localization technologies for indoor human tracking. In: 2010 5th International Conference on Future Information Technology, pp. 1–6. IEEE (2010). https://doi.org/10.1109/FUTURETECH.2010.5482731

A Time Series Forecasting Method Using DBN and Adam Optimization

Takashi Kuremoto[1]([✉]), Masafumi Furuya[2], Shingo Mabu[2], and Kunikazu Kobayashi[3]

[1] Nippon Institute of Technology, Saitama 345-8501, Japan
kuremoto.takashi@nit.ac.jp
[2] Yamaguchi University, Yamaguchi 755-8611, Japan
[3] Aichi Prefectural University, Aich 480-1342, Japan

Abstract. Deep Belief Net (DBN) was applied to the field of time series forecasting in our early works. In this paper, we propose to adopt Adaptive Moment Estimation (Adam) optimization method to the fine-tuning process of DBN instead of the conventional Error Back-Propagation (BP) method. Meta parameters, such as the number of layers of Restricted Boltzmann Machine (RBM), the number of units in each layer, the learning rate, are optimized by Random Search (RS) or Particle Swarm Optimization (PSO). Comparison experiments showed the priority of the proposed method in both cases of a benchmark dataset CATS which is an artificial time series data used in competitions for long-term forecasting, and Lorenz chaos for short-term forecasting in the sense not only prediction precision but also learning performance.

Keywords: Time series forecasting · Deep learning · Deep Belief Net · Error Back-Propagation · Adam learning optimization

1 Introduction

The study of time series forecasting benefits to many fields, such as the prediction of electricity consumption, stock prices, population, amount of rainfall, and so on. Generally, there are two kinds of theories of time series forecasting: linear models, and non-linear models. The former includes Auto-Regressive (AR), Moving Average (MA), and a combination of them ARIMA. For the effect to financial and economic fields, the proposer of Auto-Regressive Conditional Heteroskedasticity (ARCH) [1], R. Engle was awarded by Nobel Memorial Prize in Economic Sciences in 2003. The later, non-linear methods, usually utilize artificial neural networks such as Multi-Layered Perceptron (MLP), Radial Basis Function Net (RBFN), and deep learning methods [2–6].

In our previous works [3–6], Deep Belief Net (DBN) [7], a well-known deep learning model, was firstly applied to the time series forecasting. And a hybrid model with DBN and ARIMA was also proposed to improve the prediction precision [8, 9]. The hybrid model was a combination of Artificial Neural Networks (ANN) and linear models which is inspired by the theory of G.P. Zhang [10].

Y. Kambayashi et al. (Eds.): AICON 2022, LNICST 477, pp. 95–106, 2023.
https://doi.org/10.1007/978-3-031-29126-5_8

Generally, error Back-Propagation (BP) [11], is used as the training method (optimization) of ANNs. Meanwhile, recently, Adaptive Moment Estimation (Adam) [12], an advanced gradient descent algorithm of BP, is widely utilized in the training of deep neural networks. The concept of Adam is to adopt the first-order momentum, i.e., the past gradient, and the second-order momentum, i.e., the absolute gradient, into the update process of parameters. By considering the average gradient, Adam overcomes the local extremum problem in the high dimensional parameter space, and tackles non-stationary objectives.

In this study, Adam is firstly adopted to the fine-tuning process of DBN instead of the conventional BP optimization method. Benchmark dataset CATS [13, 14], an artificial time series data utilized in time series forecasting competition, and a chaotic time series given by Lorenz chaos which is a famous chaotic theory for its butterfly attractor, were used in the comparison experiment. In both experiments, DBN with Adam showed its priority to the conventional BP method in the fine-tuning process.

2 DBN for Time Series Forecasting

The original Deep Belief Net [7] was proposed for dimension reduction and image classification. It is a kind of deep auto-encoder which composed by multiple Restricted Boltzmann Machines (RBMs). For time series forecasting, the part of decoder of DBN is replaced by a feedforward ANN, Multi-Layered Perceptron (MLP) in our previous works [5, 6]. The structure of the DBN is shown in Fig. 1.

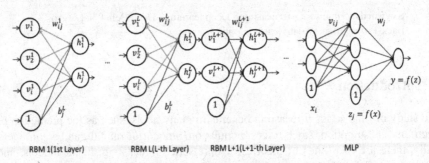

Fig. 1. A structure of a DBN composed by RBMs and MLP [6, 8, 9].

2.1 RBM and Its Learning Rule

Restricted Boltzmann Machine (RBM) [7] is a kind of Hopfield neural network but with 2 layers. Units in the visible layer connect to the units in the hidden layer with different weights. The outputs of units v_i, h_j are binary, i.e., 0 or 1, except the initial value of visible units is given by the input data. The probabilities of 1 of a visible unit and a hidden unit are according to the following.

$$p(h_j = 1|v) = \frac{1}{1 + exp(-b_j - \sum_{i=1}^{n} w_{ji} v_i)} \tag{1}$$

$$p(v_i = 1|h) = \frac{1}{1 + exp(-b_i - \sum_{j=1}^{m} w_{ij} h_j)} \qquad (2)$$

Here b_i, b_j, w_{ij} are the biases and the weights of units. The learning rules of RBM are given as follows.

$$\Delta w_{ij} = \varepsilon(< v_i h_j >_{\text{data}} - < v_i h_j >_{\text{model}}) \qquad (3)$$

$$\Delta b_i = \varepsilon(< v_i > - < \tilde{v}_i >) \qquad (4)$$

$$\Delta b_j = \varepsilon(< h_j > - < \tilde{h}_j >) \qquad (5)$$

where $0 < \varepsilon < 1$ is a learning rate, $p_{ij} = < v_i h_j >_{\text{data}}$, $p'_{ij} < v_i h_j >_{\text{model}}$, $< v_i >$, $< h_j >$ indicate the first Gibbs sampling ($k = 0$) and $< \tilde{v}_i >$, $< \tilde{h}_j >$ are the expectations after the kth Gibbs sampling, and it also works when $k = 1$.

2.2 MLP and Its Learning Rule

A feedforward neural network Multi-Layered Perceptron (MLP) [11] inspired the second Artificial Intelligence (AI) boom in 1980s (see Fig. 1). The input x_i ($i = 1, 2, ...n$) is fired by the unit z_j with connection weight v_{ji} in a hidden layer by an activation function, and also the output $y = f(z)$ is given by the function and connection weights w_j ($j = 1, 2, ...K$) as follows.

$$y = f(z) = \frac{1}{1 + exp(-\sum_{j=1}^{K+1} w_j z_j)} \qquad (6)$$

$$f(z_j) = \frac{1}{1 + exp(-\sum_{i=1}^{n+1} v_{ji} x_i)} \qquad (7)$$

where biases $x_{n+1} = 1.0$, $z_{K+1} = 1.0$.

Error Back-Propagation (BP) [11] serves as the learning rule of MLP as follows.

$$\Delta w_j = -\varepsilon(y - \tilde{y})y(1 - y)z_j \qquad (8)$$

$$\Delta v_{ji} = -\varepsilon(y - \tilde{y})y(1 - y)w_j z_j(1 - z_j)x_i \qquad (9)$$

where $0 < \varepsilon < 1$ is the learning rate, $\tilde{y}$ is the teacher signal, i.e., the value of training sample.

Meanwhile, because the BP method is sensitive to the noise and easy to convergence to the local minimum, it is modified by Adam (adaptive moment) proposed by Kingma and Ba in 2014 [12].

$$\Delta\theta_t = \frac{\widehat{m}_t}{\varepsilon + \sqrt{\widehat{v}_t}} \tag{10}$$

$$\widehat{m}_t = \frac{\beta_1^t m_{t-1}}{1 - \beta_1^t} + g_t \tag{11}$$

$$\widehat{v}_t = \frac{\beta_2^t v_{t-1}}{1 - \beta_2^t} + {g_t}^2 \tag{12}$$

$$g_t = \nabla_\theta E_t(\theta_{t-1}) \tag{13}$$

where $\theta = (v_{ji}, w_j)$ is the parameter to be modified, $0 < \varepsilon, \beta_1^t, \beta_2^t < 1$ are hyper parameters and given by empirical scalar values. $E_t(\theta_{t-1})$ is the loss function, e.g., the mean squared error between the output of the network and the teacher signal.

Although Adam is the major optimization method of deep learning recently, it is not adopted to the fine-tuning of DBN for time series forecasting as we know. In study, it is proposed that Eqs. (10–13) replace Eqs. (6–9) for Eq. (3–5), e.g., the learning rules in fine-tuning process of DBN are given by Adam instead of the BP method.

2.3 Meta Parameter Optimization

To design the structure of the ANNs, the evolutional algorithm of swarm intelligence, i.e., the Particle Swarm Optimization (PSO) or the heuristic algorithm Random Search (RS) [15], are more effective than the empirical methods such as grid search algorithm [16]. In this study, PSO and RS are adopted to optimize the meta parameters of DBN, i.e., the number of RBMs, the number of units in each RBM, the number of units of MLP, the learning rate of RBMs, and the learning rates. Detail algorithms can be found in [16], and they are omitted here.

3 Experiments and Analysis

To investigate the performance of DBN with Adam optimization algorithm, comparison experiments of time series forecasting were carried out. A benchmark dataset CATS [13, 14] (see Fig. 2), which is an artificial time series dataset utilized in time series forecasting competition, and a chaotic time series of Lorenz chaos (see Fig. 6), were used in the experiments.

3.1 Benchmark CATS

CATS time series data is an artificial benchmark data for forecasting competition with ANN methods [13, 14]. This artificial time series is given with 5,000 data, among which 100 are missed (hidden by competition the organizers) (see Fig. 2). The missed data exist in 5 blocks:

- elements 981 to 1,000
- elements 1,981 to 2,000
- elements 2,981 to 3,000
- elements 3,981 to 4,000
- elements 4,981 to 5,000

The mean square error E_1 is used as the prediction precision in the competition, and it is computed by the 100 missing data and their predicted values as following:

$$E_1 = \{ \sum_{t=981}^{1000} (y_t - \bar{y}_t)^2 + \sum_{t=1981}^{2000} (y_t - \bar{y}_t)^2 + \sum_{t=2981}^{3000} (y_t - \bar{y}_t)^2 + \sum_{t=3981}^{4000} (y_t - \bar{y}_t)^2 + \sum_{t=4981}^{5000} (y_t - \bar{y}_t)^2) \}/100 \quad (14)$$

where $\bar{y}_t$ is the long-term prediction result of the missed data.

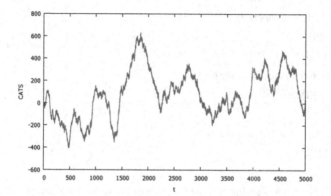

Fig. 2. A benchmark dataset CATS [13, 14].

3.2 Results and Analysis of CATS Forecasting

The meta parameter space searched by heuristic algorithms, i.e., Particle Swarm Optimization (PSO) and Random Search (RS) has 5 dimensions: the number of RBMs in DBN, the number of units of each RBM, the number of units in hidden layer of MLP, the learning rate of RBMs, the learning rate of MLP. The exploration ranges of these meta parameters are shown in Table 1.

The iteration of exploration of PSO and RS was set by convergence of evaluation functions or limitations of 2,000 in pre-training (RBM), and 10,000 in the fine-tuning (MLP). Additionally, the exploration finished when the forecasting error (mean squared error between the real data and the output of DBN) of validation data increased than the last time.

Table 1. Meta parameter ranges of exploration by PSO and RS.

Dimension	Range
The number of RBMs	0–3
The number of units in each RBM	2–20
The number of units in hidden layer of MLP	2–20
The learning rate of RBMs (pre-training)	10^{-1}–10^{-5}
The learning rate of MLP (fine-tuning)	10^{-1}–10^{-5}

Table 2. The comparison of long-term prediction precision by E_1 measurement between different methods using CATS data [13, 14].

Method	E_1
DBN (Adam + RS) (proposed)	*134.04*
DBN (Adam + PSO) (proposed)	*148.24*
DBN (BP + RS) [5]	155.53
DBN (BP + PSO) [5]	155.65
DBN(SGA) (reinforcement learning)[6]	170
DBN(BP) + ARIMA [8] [9]	244
DBN(BP)[6]	257
Kalman Smoother (The best of IJCNN '04) [14]	408
DBN[3] [4] (2 RBMs)	1215
MLP[2]	1245
A hierarchical Bayesian Learning Scheme for Autoregressive Neural Networks (The worst of IJCNN '04) [14]	1247
ARIMA[2]	1715
ARIMA + MLP(BP)[8] [9]	2153
ARIMA + DBN (BP)[8] [9]	2266

The forecasting precisions of different ANN and hybrid methods are shown in Table 2. It can be confirmed that the proposed methods, DBN using Adam fine-tuning algorithm with RS or PSO, ranked on the top of all methods. The learning curves of the proposed method (Adam adopted) and the conventional method (BP) are shown in Fig. 3 (the case of the 1st block of CATS). The convergence of loss (MSE) in Adam showed faster and smaller than the case of BP in both PSO and RS algorithms.

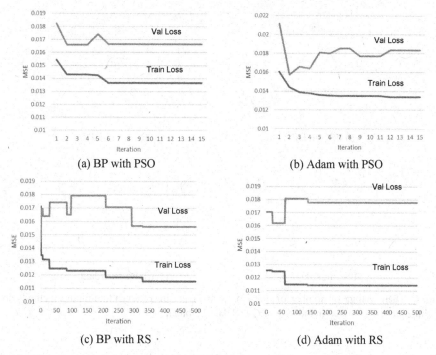

(a) BP with PSO

(b) Adam with PSO

(c) BP with RS

(d) Adam with RS

Fig. 3. The convergence of loss (MSE) of DBN in different fine-tuning processes (PSO and RS) and optimization algorithms (BP and Adam) using CATS data 1st block.

The change of the number of units in each RBM according to the different exploration algorithms, PSO and RS, is shown in Fig. 4. The iteration time of PSO ended at 15, and 500 for RS. Both exploration results showed that 2 RBMs were the best structure of DBN for the 1st block of CATS.

The change of the learning rates of different RBMs (pre-training) and MLP (fine-tuning) is shown in Fig. 5. The convergence of the learning rates were not obtained in each case of BP and Adam with PSO or RS.

The exploration results of meta parameters for the 1st block data of CATS are described in Table 3.

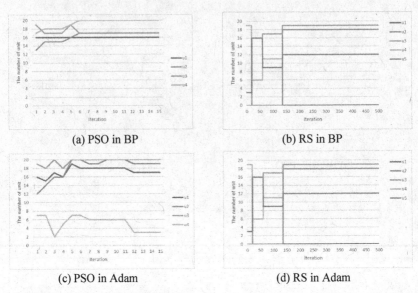

(a) PSO in BP

(b) RS in BP

(c) PSO in Adam

(d) RS in Adam

Fig. 4. Then change of number of units in RBM layers in different fine-tuning methods and optimization algorithms (in the case of CATS data 1st block).

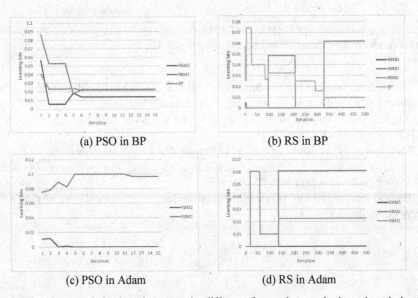

(a) PSO in BP

(b) RS in BP

(c) PSO in Adam

(d) RS in Adam

Fig. 5. The change of the learning rates in different fine-tuning methods and optimization algorithms (the case of CATS data 1st block).

Table 3. Meta parameters of DBN optimized by PSO and RS for the CATS data (Block 1)

	Adam + PSO	BP + PSO	Adam + RS	BP + RS
The number of RBMs	2	2	2	1
Learning rates of RBMs	0.0001, 0.09679	0.01392, 0.02266	0.0609, 0.0227	0.0617
Structure of DBN (the number of neurons in each layer)	17-19-20-3-1	16-17-17-20-1	18-19-12-12-1	17-5-9-1
Learning rate of MLP	Variable	0.02170	Variable	0.00951

3.3 Chaotic Time Series Data

Chaotic time series are difficult to be predicted in the case of long-term forecasting [5]. Here, we used Lorenz chaos to compare the performance of DBNs with different fine-tuning methods in the case of short-term forecasting (one-ahead forecasting). Lorenz chaos is given by 3-D differential equations as follows.

$$\begin{cases} \frac{dx}{dt} = -\sigma \cdot x + \sigma \cdot y \\ \frac{dy}{dt} = -x \cdot z + r \cdot x - y \\ \frac{dz}{dt} = x \cdot y - b \cdot z \end{cases} \tag{15}$$

where parameters are given by $\sigma = 10$, $b = 28$, $r = \frac{8}{3}$, $\Delta t = 0.01$ in the experiment. The attract of Lorenz chaos, a butterfly aspect, and the time series of x-axis are shown in Fig. 6.

3.4 Results and Analysis of Chaotic Time Series Forecasting

The exploration results of meta parameters for Lorenz chaotic time series by PSO and RS in different fine-tuning methods (Adam and BP) are described in Table 4. Adam learning rules resulted deeper structure of DBN than PSO, especially in the case of RS. The convergence of loss (MSE) of DBN in different fine-tuning processes (BP and Adam) and optimization algorithms (PSO and RS) using the time series data of Lorenz chaos (1 to 1000 in x-axis) is shown in Fig. 7. And finally, the precisions of different forecasting methods are compared by Table 5. The best method for this time series forecasting was Adam with PSO, which yielded the lowest loss 1.68×10^{-5}.

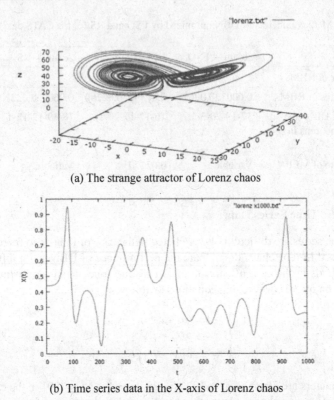

(a) The strange attractor of Lorenz chaos

(b) Time series data in the X-axis of Lorenz chaos

Fig. 6. Lorenz chaos used in the short-term (one-ahead) prediction experiment.

Table 4. Meta parameters of DBN optimized by PSO and RS for the Lorenz chaos (x-axis).

	Adam + PSO	BP + PSO	Adam + RS	BP + RS
The number of RBMs	2	2	3	1
Learning rates of RBMs	0.01626, 0.00001	0.0949, 0.04120	0.08818, 0.02499, 0.03891	0.0659
Structure of DBN (the number of neurons in each layer)	20-20-7-2-1	6-6-10-10-1	3-9-13-12-12-2-1	20-19-10-1
Learning rate of MLP	Variable	0.0302	Variable	0.0820

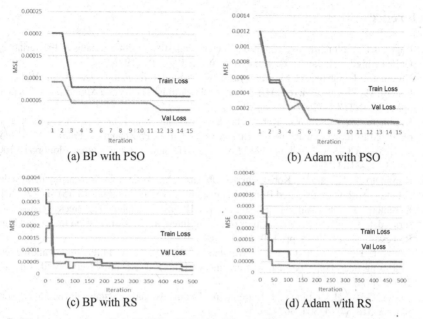

Fig. 7. The convergence of loss (MSE) of DBN in different fine-tuning processes (BP and Adam) and optimization algorithms (PSO and RS) using the time series data of Lorenz chaos (1 to 1000 in x-axis).

Table 5. Precisions (MSE) of different DBNs (upper: training error; lower: test error).

Exploration	BP ($\times 10^{-5}$)	Adam ($\times 10^{-5}$)
RS	**3.32**	5.19
	1.70	3.03
PSO	5.95	**3.23**
	2.86	*1.68*

4 Conclusions

An improved gradient descent method Adam was firstly adopted to the fine-tuning process of the Deep Belief Net (DBN) for time series forecasting in this study. The effectiveness of the novel optimization algorithm showed its priority not only for the benchmark dataset CATS which was a long-term forecasting given by five blocks of artificial data, but also for the chaotic time series data which was a short-term forecasting (one-ahead) problem. As the optimizer Adam has been improved to be Nadam, AdaSecant, AMSGrad, AdaBound, etc., new challenges are remained in the future works.

Acknowledgement. This work was supported by JSPS KAKENHI Grant No. 22H03709, and No. 22K12152.

References

1. Engle, R.F.: Autoregressive conditional heteroscedasticity with estimates of the variance of United Kingdom inflation. Econometrica **50**(4), 987–1007 (1982)
2. Kuremoto, T., Obayashi, M., Kobayashi, K.: Neural forecasting systems. In: Weber, C., Elshaw, M., Mayer, N.M. (eds.) Reinforcement Learning, Theory and Applications, Chapter 1, pp. 1–20, INTECH (2008)
3. Kuremoto, T., Kimura, S., Kobayashi, K., Obayashi, M.: Time series forecasting using restricted Boltzmann machine. In: Huang, D.-S., Gupta, P., Zhang, X., Premaratne, P. (eds.) ICIC 2012. CCIS, vol. 304, pp. 17–22. Springer, Heidelberg (2012). https://doi.org/10.1007/978-3-642-31837-5_3
4. Kuremoto, T., Kimura, S., Kobayashi, K., Obayashi, M.: Time series forecasting using a deep belief network with restricted Boltzmann machines. Neurocomputing **137**(5), 47–56 (2014)
5. Kuremoto, T., Obayashi, M., Kobayashi, K., Hirata, T., Mabu, S.: Forecast chaotic time series data by DBNs. In: Proceedings of the 7th International Congress on Image and Signal Processing (CISP 2014), pp. 1304–1309 (2014)
6. Hirata, T., Kuremoto, T., Obayashi, M., Mabu, S., Kobayashi, K.: Forecasting real time series data using deep belief net and reinforcement learning. J. Robotics Netw. Artif. Life **4**(4), 260–264 (2018)
7. Hinton, G.E., Salakhutdinov, R.R.: Reducing the dimensionality of data with neural networks. Science **313**(5786), 504–507 (2006)
8. Hirata, T., Kuremoto, T., Obayashi, M., Mabu, S., Kobayashi, K.: Time series prediction using DBN and ARIMA. In: International Conference on Computer Application Technologies (CCATS 2015), pp. 24–29. Matsue, Japan (2015)
9. Hirata, T., Kuremoto, T., Obayashi, M., Mabu, S., Kobayashi, K.: A novel approach to time series forecasting using deep learning and linear model. IEEJ Trans. Electron. Inf. Syst. **136**(3), 348–356 (2016)
10. Zhang, G.P.: Time series forecasting using a hybrid ARIMA and neural network model. Neurocomputing **50**, 159–175 (2003)
11. Rumelhart, D.E., Hinton, G.E., Williams, R.J.: Learning representations by back-propagating errors. Nature **323**(6088), 533–536 (1986)
12. Kingma, D.P., Ba, J.: Adam: a method for stochastic optimization. arXiv preprint arXiv:1412.6980 (2014)
13. Lendasse, A., Oja, E., Simula, O., Verleysen, M.: Time series prediction competition: the CATS benchmark. In: Proceedings of International Joint Conference on Neural Networks (IJCNN 2004), pp. 1615–1620 (2004)
14. Lendasse, A., Oja, E., Simula, O., Verleysen, M.: Time series prediction competition: the CATS benchmark. Neurocomputing **70**(13–15), 2325–2329 (2007)
15. Bergstra, J., Bengio, Y.: Random search for hyper-parameter optimization. J. Mach. Learn. Res. **13**(2), 281–305 (2012)
16. Kuremoto, T., Hirata, T., Obayashi, M., Kobayashi, K., Mabu, S.: Search heuristics for the optimization of DBN for time series forecasting. In: Iba, H., Noman, N. (eds.) Deep Neural Evolution. NCS, pp. 131–152. Springer, Singapore (2020). https://doi.org/10.1007/978-981-15-3685-4_5

Unity-Bounded Function and Benchmark Design Specifications Targeted for Designing Typical Variable Digital Filters

Tian-Bo Deng[✉]

Department of Information Science, Faculty of Science, Toho University, Miyama 2-2-1, Funabashi, Chiba 274-8510, Japan
deng@is.sci.toho-u.ac.jp

Abstract. This paper first presents a set of benchmark design specifications that include variable lowpass specification, variable highpass specification, variable bandpass specification, variable bandstop specification, and variable notch specification. The design specifications are targeted for testing and verifying the effectiveness of various newly developed algorithms for designing typical variable digital filters. The paper then provides a novel unity-bounded function developed for guaranteeing the stability of a recursive variable transfer function. Finally, demonstrative results using one of the benchmark design specifications and the unity-bounded function are illustrated.

Keywords: Variable digital filter (VDF) · Benchmark specification · Typical filter · Unity-bounded function · Amplitude response · Recursive VDF · Stability

1 Introduction

Digital filters play extremely important roles in a vast number of fields such as signal processing, speech processing, image processing, automatic control, digital communications, and other information technology (IT) and artificial-intelligence (AI)-related fields. If the coefficients of a digital filter are fixed, the frequency-domain property of such a filter is also fixed. Indeed, many practical applications necessitate tunable frequency-domain responses (properties) during filtering process. The digital filter with frequency-response tunability is called variable digital filter (VDF). To tune the frequency response, one can parameterize the VDF coefficients as functions of the parameters that are used to tune the frequency response. Through simply varying the values of VDF coefficients, one can update the frequency response. In other words, a VDF has the coefficients that are usually the functions of the parameters that are used to vary the frequency response. As an example, a parameter may be used to tune the bandwidths of a VDF. For simplicity, this paper only discusses the simplest case with only a single parameter.

A VDF may have variable fractional delay [1–8], and such a VDF has unity amplitude. This paper deals with the VDFs that have tunable amplitude responses [9–15], and

Y. Kambayashi et al. (Eds.): AICON 2022, LNICST 477, pp. 107–120, 2023.
https://doi.org/10.1007/978-3-031-29126-5_9

summarizes two major contributions. The first key point is to present a set of typical benchmark design specifications (amplitude specifications) that are spefically developed for VDF designs. Those benchmark design specifications include variable lowpass specification, variable highpass specification, variable bandpass specification, variable bandstop specification, and variable notch-frequency specification. Such typical design specifications are targeted for the design of various typical VDFs, including variable lowpass filter, variable highpass filter, variable bandpass filter, variable bandstop filter, and variable notch-frequency filter. In other words, the major objective of this paper is to present those basic design specifications such that the filter designer can take any of them as a benchmark design specification for testing and verifying the effectiveness of various developed VDF design algorithms. This paper also aims to present a new function called unity-bounded function, which can be employed in guaranteeing the stability of recursive VDFs [10, 15]. Employing the unity-bounded function ensures that the filter designer is able to get a recursive VDF with guaranteed stability. That is, the resulting transfer function is an absolutely stabilized mathematical model for a recursive VDF. Finally, both the presented benchmark design specifications and the new unity bounded function is used to design recursive digital filters with various bandwidths. The computer simulation results verify that the developed unity-bounded function is useful in getting high-performance recursive digital filters with variable bandwidths. Furthermore, the designed recursive digital filters with different bandwidths are stable.

2 Typical Benchmark Specifications

A recursive VDF can be described by using the mathematical model (transfer function)

$$H(z, \rho) = \frac{\sum_{k=0}^{N} a_k(\rho)z^{-k}}{\prod_{k=1}^{N/2} \left[1 + b_{k,1}(\rho)z^{-k} + b_{k,2}(\rho)z^{-2}\right]}. \tag{1}$$

As long as a VDF that has variable amplitude response is concerned, its frequency bandwidths are variable. In (1), ρ is a parameter utilized for changing the bandwidths of $H(z, \rho)$, and the coefficients of $H(z, \rho)$ are not constant, but the functions of ρ. For simplicity, the parameter ρ is called the bandwith (BW)-tuning parameter. Although we discuss only one parameter ρ in this paper, the idea in this paper can be readily generalized to the case where a VDF has the coefficients parameterized as the functions of multi-parameters.

As mentioned above, all the coefficients $a_k(\rho)$, $b_{k,1}(\rho)$, and $b_{k,2}(\rho)$ are the functions of the BW-tuning parameter ρ. Once $a_k(\rho)$, $b_{k,1}(\rho)$, and $b_{k,2}(\rho)$ are determined, one can change the values of ρ and thus get the new values of the coefficients $a_k(\rho)$, $b_{k,1}(\rho)$, $b_{k,2}(\rho)$, which leads to the changes of the bandwidths of $H(z, \rho)$.

Assume that the desired (ideal) amplitude response $A_d(\omega, \rho)$ is given. The objective of designing a VDF is to determine the optimal functions $a_k(\rho)$, $b_{k,1}(\rho)$, and $b_{k,2}(\rho)$ in such a manner that the desired amplitude response $A_d(\omega, \rho)$ is best approximated through minimizing a specifically defined error function. That is, the problem is about how to find the optimal functions $a_k(\rho)$, $b_{k,1}(\rho)$, and $b_{k,2}(\rho)$. The next subsection provides a set of typical amplitude design specifications that can be taken as benchmark specifications in designing various typical VDFs. The utilizations of those typical design specifications facilitate the VDF designers to evaluate various newly developed design techniques.

2.1 Variable Lowpass Design Specification

Let us consider the first design specification defined by

$$A_d(\omega, \rho) = \begin{cases} 1, & \omega \in [0, \omega_p] \\ 0, & \omega \in [\omega_s, \pi] \end{cases} \tag{2}$$

where the normalized radian frequency is $\omega [0, \pi]$, and ω_p and ω_s denote the passband-edge frequency and stopband-edge frequency, respectively,

$$\omega_p = 0.30\pi + \rho$$
$$\omega_s = 0.40\pi + \rho.$$

It is clear that this design specification is a variable lowpass amplitude, and both ω_p and ω_s can be tuned by using the single BW-tuning parameter

$$\rho \in [-0.10\pi, 0.10\pi].$$

This lowpass design specification is illustrated in Fig. 1, where both the passband width and the stopband width are variable, but the transition bandwidth is not variable (fixed at 0.10π).

2.2 Variable Highpass Design Specification

Next, let us consider the highpass design specification defined by

$$A_d(\omega, \rho) = \begin{cases} 0, & \omega \in [0, \omega_s] \\ 1, & \omega \in [\omega_p, \pi] \end{cases} \tag{3}$$

where ω_s and ω_p are stopband-edge frequency and passband-edge frequency, respectively,

$$\omega_s = 0.60\pi + \rho$$
$$\omega_p = 0.70\pi + \rho.$$

Similar to the above lowpass design specification, both ω_s and ω_p can be varied via changing the value of the single BW-tuning parameter

$$\rho \in [-0.10\pi, 0.10\pi].$$

Figure 2 shows the variable highpass amplitude specification, where the BW-tuning parameter ρ tunes passband width and stopband width, while the transition bandwidth remains fixed (0.10π).

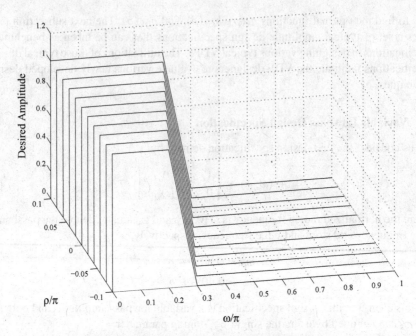

Fig. 1. Variable lowpass design specification

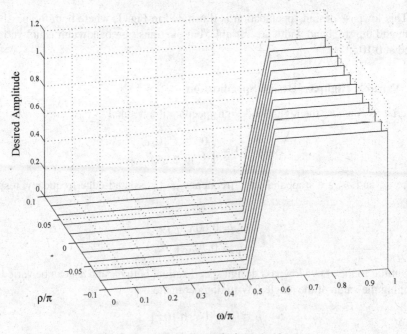

Fig. 2. Variable highpass design specification

2.3   Variable Bandpass Design Specification

The third one is the bandpass amplitude design specification defined by

$$A_s(\omega, \rho) = \begin{cases} 0, & \omega \in [0, \omega_{s1}] \\ 1, & \omega \in \left[\omega_{p1}, \omega_{p2}\right] \\ 0, & \omega \in [\omega_2, \pi] \end{cases} \tag{4}$$

where ω_{p1} and ω_{p2} denote two passband-edge frequencies, and ω_{s1}, ω_{s2} specify two stopband-edge frequencies. Those band-edge frequencies are defined by

$$\omega_{s1} = 0.25\pi + \rho$$
$$\omega_{p1} = 0.35\pi + \rho$$
$$\omega_{p2} = 0.65\pi - \rho$$
$$\omega_{s2} = 0.75\pi - \rho$$

and the BW-tuning parameter is

$$\rho \in [-0.10\pi, 0.10\pi].$$

Figure 3 shows this variable bandpass design specification. Here, the two transition band- widths are also fixed (0.10π), while the passband width and stopband widths can be tuned through changing the value of parameter ρ.

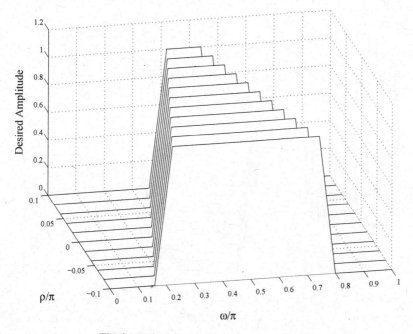

Fig. 3. Variable bandpass design specification

2.4 Variable Bandstop Design Specification

The next one is the bandstop design specification defined by

$$A_d(\omega, \rho) = \begin{cases} 0, & \omega \in [0, \omega_{p1}] \\ 1, & \omega \in [\omega_{s1}, \omega_{s2}] \\ 0, & \omega \in [\omega_{p2}, \pi] \end{cases} \qquad (5)$$

where ω_{p1}, ω_{p2} denote two passband-edge frequencies, and ω_{s1}, ω_{s2} denote two stopband-edge frequencies. Those band-edge frequencies are defined by

$$\omega_{p1} = 0.25\pi + \rho$$
$$\omega_{s1} = 0.35\pi + \rho$$
$$\omega_{s2} = 0.65\pi - \rho$$
$$\omega_{p2} = 0.75\pi - \rho.$$

Similarly, the above band-edge frequencies are tuned by

$$\rho \in [-0.10\pi, \ 0.10\pi].$$

Figure 4 illustrates this variable bandstop design specification, where the two pass-band widths and one stopband width are tuned by using ρ, while the two transition band-widths keep constant (0.10π).

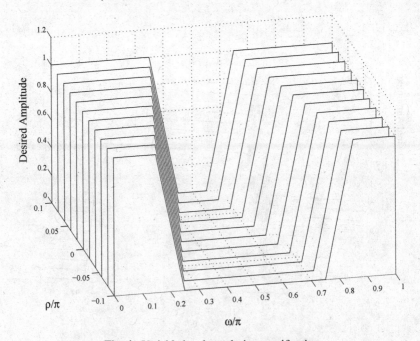

Fig. 4. Variable bandstop design specification

2.5   Variable Notch-Frequency Design Specification

Finally, let us consider the variable notch-frequency design specification defined by

$$A_d(\omega, \rho) = \begin{cases} 0, & \omega \in [0, \omega_{p1}] \\ 1, & \omega = \omega_s \\ 0, & \omega \in [\omega_{p2}, \pi] \end{cases} \tag{6}$$

where ω_{p1}, ω_{p2} are two passband-edge frequencies, and ω_s is the notch frequency. The band-edge frequencies are defined by

$$\omega_{p1} = 0.40\pi + \rho$$
$$\omega_s = 0.50\pi + \rho$$
$$\omega_{p2} = 0.60\pi + \rho$$

with

$$\rho \in [-0.10\pi, 0.10\pi].$$

Figure 5 shows this variable notch-frequency design specification. The notch frequency can be tuned by using the notch-tuning parameter ρ, while the two transition bandwidths are fixed at 0.10π.

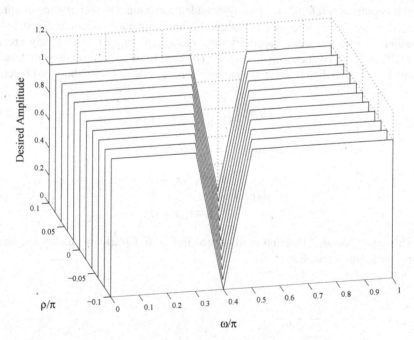

Fig. 5. Variable notch-frequency design specification

3　Unity-Bounded Function

The recursive VDF in (1) is stable if and only if the stability condition

$$\begin{cases} \left|b_{k,2}(\rho) < 1\right| \\ \left|b_{k,1}(\rho) < 1 + b_{k,2}(\rho)\right| \end{cases} \tag{7}$$

is satisfied. Obviously, only the denominator coefficients $b_{k,2}(\rho)$, $b_{k,1}(\rho)$ determine whether or not the recursive VDF is stable. To guarantee the stability, an effective way is to transform denominator coefficients $b_{k,2}(\rho)$, $b_{k,1}(\rho)$ into the form

$$\begin{cases} b_{k,2}(\rho) = \beta \cdot U\left(x_{k,2}(\rho)\right) \\ b_{k,1}(\rho) = \beta \cdot U\left(x_{k,1}(\rho)\right)\left(1 + b_{k,2}(\rho)\right) \end{cases} \tag{8}$$

where

$$0 < \beta < 1$$

and $U(x)$ is a transformation function called unity-bounded function. The unity-bounded function exhibits the feature

$$U(x) \in [-1, \ 1] \tag{9}$$

and this condition is referred to as unity-bounded condition. One can rigorously (theoretically) prove that as long as $U(x)$ meets this unity-bounded condition, the stability, condition (7) is always met for arbitrary functions $x_{k,2}(\rho)$, $x_{k,1}(\rho)$. In designing a recursive VDF, the optimal functions $x_{k,2}(\rho)$, $x_{k,1}(\rho)$ need to be found, and they are usually assumed to be the polynomials in the parameter ρ. Here, a new unity-bounded function

$$U_x = \begin{cases} x, & |x| \leq 1 \\ \text{sign}(x), & |x| > 1 \end{cases} \tag{10}$$

is developed, where the sign function $\text{sign}(x)$ is defined as

$$\text{sign}(x) = \begin{cases} 1, & x > 0 \\ 0, & x = 0 \\ -1, & x < 0 \end{cases} \tag{11}$$

This unity-bounded function is illustrated in Fig. 6. Clearly, it satisfies the unity-bounded condition specified in (9).

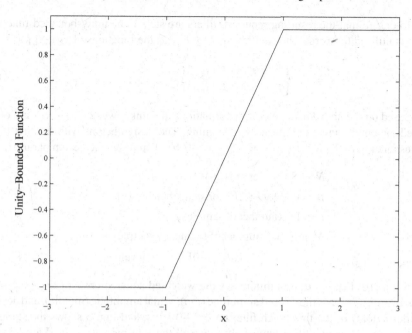

Fig. 6. Unity-bounded function $U(x)$

4 An Illustrative Example

In this section, the proposed unity-bounded function $U(x)$ in Fig. 6 is employed in designing a set of recursive digital filters for approximating the discretized notch specifications shown in Fig. 5, where each curve represents a discretized design specification associated with a sampled value of ρ. Although the variable notch specification in (6) is continuously tunable, this paper only deals with the approximations of the discretized notch specifications in Fig. 5, where the parameter ρ takes discretized values ρ_i, $i = 1$, $2, , I$, and $I = 11$. Each curve in Fig. 5 represents a design specification with a different notch-frequency, and each of them is separately approximated by using an individual transfer function

$$H(z) = \frac{\sum\limits_{k=0}^{N} a_k z^{-k}}{\prod\limits_{k=1}^{N/2} \left[1 + b_{k,1} z^{-1} + b_{k,2} z^{-2}\right]}. \tag{12}$$

To ensure that the resulting recursive filters are stable, the unity-bounded function $U(x)$ is utilized to express the coefficients $b_{k,2}$, $b_{k,1}$ as the functions of $x_{k,2}$, $x_{k,1}$ as

$$\begin{cases} b_{k,2} = \beta \cdot U(x_k, 2) \\ b_{k,1} = \beta \cdot U(x_{k,1})(1 + b_{k,2}). \end{cases} \tag{13}$$

Based on the above parameter transformations, the unknowns a_k, $x_{k,2}$, $x_{k,1}$ are optimized via employing a nonlinear programming. The design begins with the first filter corresponding to the first sample of ρ ($\rho_1 = -0.10\pi$), and sets the design parameters

$$N = 8 \quad \text{(order of H}(z))$$
$$\beta = 0.99999 \quad \text{(factor small than untity)}$$
$$I = 11 \quad \text{(number of samples } \rho_i)$$
$$M = 201 \quad \text{(number of frequency samples } \omega_m)$$
$$\begin{bmatrix} a_k\, x_{k,2}\, z_{k,1} \end{bmatrix} = [0\,0\,\cdots\,0] \quad \text{(inital values).}$$

As in [10–14], the design minimizes the weighted squared error of the amplitude response. Fig. 7 shows the desired amplitude (top), actual amplitude (middle), and design errors (bottom) of the first notch filter ($\rho_1 = -0.10\pi$), and Fig. 8 shows the stability triangles for this notch filter. Obviously, since all the four pairs ($b_{k,1}$, $b_{k,2}$) are located inside the stability triangles, it is concluded that the stability condition (7) is met, and the designed notch digital filter is stable.

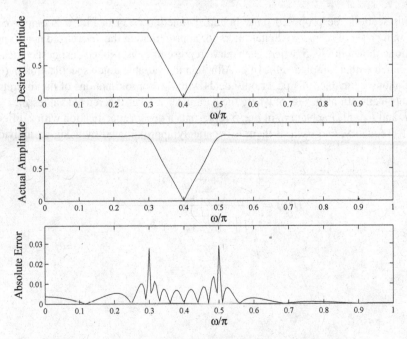

Fig. 7. Amplitude and errors of the notch filter ($\rho_1 = -0.10\pi$)

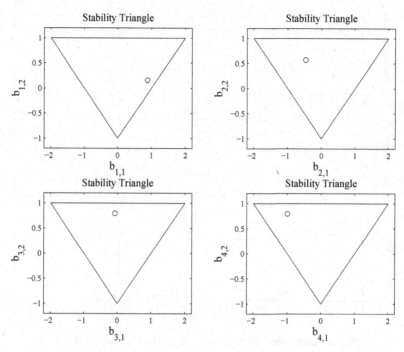

Fig. 8. Stability triangles for the notch filter ($\rho 1= -0.10\pi$)

Next, let us check the last notch filter corresponding to $\rho_{11} = 0.10\pi$. Fig. 9 shows the desired amplitude (top), actual amplitude (middle), and design errors (bottom), and Fig. 10 shows the stability triangles. Similar to the first notch filter, all the pairs ($b_{k,1}$, $b_{k,2}$) are inside the stability triangles. Therefore, this recursive notch filter is also stable.

Finally, Fig. 11 plots the amplitude responses of all the notch filters ($I = 11$), and Fig. 12 plots the loci of the pairs ($b_{k,1}$, $b_{k,2}$) when ρ changes its value from ρ_1 to ρ_{11}. Again, Fig. 12 shows that all the pairs ($b_{k,1}$, $b_{k,2}$) are inside the stability triangles, which verifies that all the obtained notch filters are stable. The mean value of the normalized root-mean-squared (RMS) errors and the mean value of the maximum errors are

$$\overline{E}_2 = 0.5208\%, \ \overline{E}_{max} = 0.0315$$

respectively. The above simulation results indicate that the developed unity-bounded function for the parameter transformations not only can guarantee the stability, but also can produce VDFs with high accuracy.

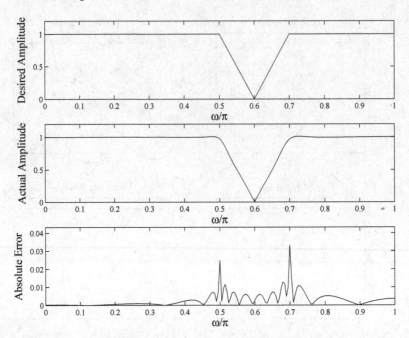

Fig. 9. Amplitude and errors of the last notch filter ($\rho_{11}= 0.10\pi$)

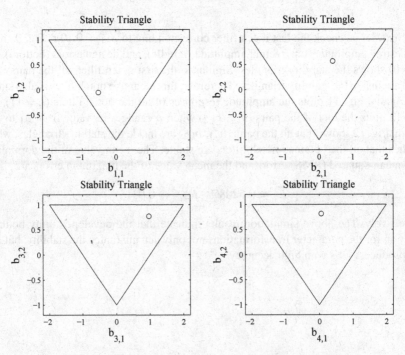

Fig. 10. Stability triangles for the last notch filter ($\rho_{11}= 0.10\pi$)

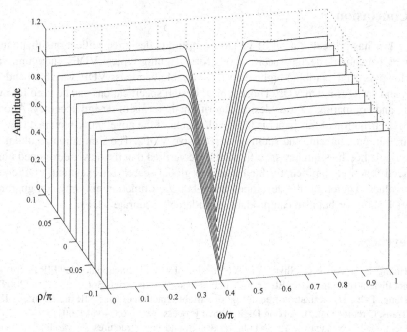

Fig. 11. Amplitude responses of all the notch filters ($I = 11$)

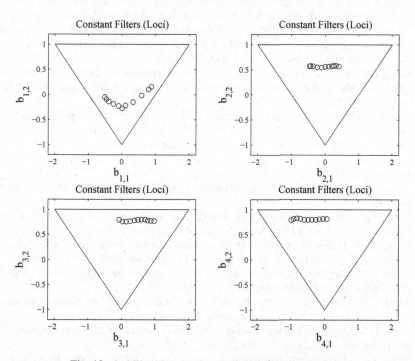

Fig. 12. Stability triangles for all the notch filters ($I = 11$)

5 Conclusion

This paper has presented a set of variable amplitude design specifications that can be taken as benchmark design specifications for designing typical VDFs, including variable lowpass VDF, variable highpass VDF, variable bandpass VDF, variable bandstop VDF, and variable notch VDF. Those typical design specifications can be used for evaluating and comparing various design algorithms in terms of design accuracy. Another major contribution of this paper is the development of the novel unity-bounded function required in guaranteeing the stability of recursive VDFs. The simulation results using the variable notch-frequency specification have verified that the newly developed unity-bounded function significantly facilitates the global search for excellent VDF coefficient values. Therefore, the developed unity-bounded function not only can guarantee the VDF stability, but also can produce considerably accurate VDFs.

References

1. Huang, Y.-D, Pei, S.-C., Shyu, J.-J.: WLS design of variable fractional-delay FIR filters using coefficient relationship. IEEE Trans. Circuits Syst. II, Exp. Briefs **56**(3), 220–224 (2009)
2. Deng, T.-B.: Discretization-free design of variable fractional-delay FIR digital filters. IEEE Trans. Circuits Syst. II, Analog Digit. Signal Process. **48**(6), 637–644 (2001)
3. Deng, T.-B., Nakagawa, Y.: SVD-based design and new structures for variable fractional-delay digital filters. IEEE Trans. Signal Process. **52**(9), 2513–2527 (2004)
4. Deng, T.-B., Lian, Y.: Weighted-least-squares design of variable fractional-delay FIR filters using coefficient-symmetry. IEEE Trans. Signal Process. **54**(8), 3023–3038 (2006)
5. Deng, T.-B.: Design and parallel implementation of FIR digital filters with simultaneously variable magnitude and non-integer phase-delay responses. IEEE Trans. Circuits Syst. II: Analog Digit. Signal Processing **50**(5), 243–250 (2003)
6. Deng, T.-B.: Closed-form design and efficient implementation of variable digital filters with simultaneously tunable magnitude and fractional-delay. IEEE Trans. Signal Process. **52**(6), 1668–1681 (2004)
7. Soontornwong, P., Chivapreecha, S.: Pascal-interpolation-based noninteger delay filter and low-complexity realization. Radioengineering **24**(4), 1002–1012 (2015)
8. Deng, T.-B.: Minimax design of low-complexity even-order variable fractional-delay filters using second-order cone programming. IEEE Trans. Circuits Syst. II: Express Briefs **58**(10), 692–696 (2011)
9. Zarour, R., Fahmy, M.M.: A design technique for variable digital filters. IEEE Trans. Circuits Syst. **36**(11), 1473–1478 (1989)
10. Deng, T.-B.: Design of recursive 1-D variable filters with guaranteed stability. IEEE Trans. Circuits Syst. II, Analog Digit. Signal Process. **44**(9), 689–695 (1997)
11. Deng, T.-B.: Design of variable 2-D linear phase recursive digital filters with guaranteed stability. IEEE Trans. Circuits Syst. I: Fundam. Theory Appl. **45**(8), 859–863 (1998)
12. Deng, T.-B.: Stability trapezoid and stability-margin analysis for the second-order recursive digital filter. Signal Process. **118**(1), 97–102 (2016)
13. Deng, T.-B.: Generalized stability-triangle for guaranteeing the stability-margin of the second-order digital filter. J. Circuits, Syst. Comput. **25**(8), 1650094 1–13 (2016)
14. Deng, T.-B.: Design of recursive variable-digital-filters with theoretically-guaranteed stability. Int. J. Electron. **103**(12), 2013–2028 (2016)
15. Deng, T.-B.: The Lp-norm-minimization design of stable variable-bandwidth digital filters. J. Circuits Syst. Comput. **27**(7), 1850102 1–18 (2018)

Evolutionary Computation

Proposal and Evaluation of a Course-Classification-Support System Emphasizing Communication with the Sub-committees Within the Committee of Validation and Examination for Degrees

Kazuteru Miyazaki[✉][ID], Syu Yamaguchi, Rie Mori, Yumiko Yoshikawa, Takanori Saito, and Toshiya Suzuki

National Institution for Academic Degrees and Quality Enhancement of Higher Education, Tokyo, Japan
{teru,yamaguti-s,rmori,yosikawa,tknrsaito,suzuki-t}@niad.ac.jp
http://www.niad.ac.jp

Abstract. The National Institution for Academic Degrees and Quality Enhancement of Higher Education (NIAD-QE) awards academic degrees based on the accumulation of credits. These credits must be classified according to pre-determined criteria for the chosen disciplinary field. This work has been carried out by the sub-committees within the *Committee of Validation and Examination for Degrees* (CVED), whose members should be well-versed in the syllabus of each course to ensure appropriate classification. The number of applicants is increasing every year, and thus, a course classification system supported by information technology is strongly desired. We have proposed the *Course Classification Support system* (CCS) and the *Active Course Classification Support system* (ACCS) for the awarding of degrees in NIAD-QE. On the other hand, in this paper, from the standpoint of emphasizing communication with the sub-committees, we construct a course classification support system using deep learning, which has been developing remarkably in recent years. We also confirm the effectiveness of the proposed method using actual syllabi from two universities.

Keywords: syllabus · course-classification · degree awarding · recommender system · deep learning

1 Introduction

NIAD-QE is an incorporated administrative agency under the Ministry of Education, Culture, Sports, Science and Technology (MEXT). NIAD-QE's missions include contributing to the development of life-long learning society by enabling learners who are not university students to earn academic degrees. Assessing

Y. Kambayashi et al. (Eds.): AICON 2022, LNICST 477, pp. 123–130, 2023.
https://doi.org/10.1007/978-3-031-29126-5_10

the results of various learning provided at the higher education level, NIAD-QE awards Bachelor's degrees to learners who have already acquired sufficient number of academic credits to make sufficient academic achievements in the particular disciplinary field.

In this degree-awarding process, an applicant who wishes to earn a degree from NIAD-QE must classify courses he/she took according to pre-determined criteria in each disciplinary field, being publicized in the guidebook called *Alternative Routes to a Bachelor's Degree* (https://www.niad.ac.jp/media/005/202202/gakushi_annai.pdf). Validity of applicants' course classifications are judged by sub-committees of CVED whose members are university professors in each field. Those judgements are made by sub-committee members based on syllabi: It is examined whether the classification by the applicant is appropriate or not. NIAD-QE awards Bachelor's degrees to about 2,500 applicants each year. One challenge is that the examination of syllabus of each course is significantly time-consuming.

It has been, therefore, desired to reduce the workload in examining syllabi without compromising the accuracy of judgement since syllabi are important material for assessments in academic areas. The focus of our research is to classify individual syllabus based on its content by utilizing information technology for the degree-awarding process at NIAD-QE. For this purpose, we have proposed CCS [6] and ACCS [7]. Following up those attempts, in this paper, we propose a method using the deep learning that emphasizes communication with the sub-committee for better results.

2   Degree-Awarding of NIAD-QE and the Course-Classification-Support System

NIAD-QE's awards academic degrees in two schemes: One is based on the successful completion of a junior college program (or its equivalent) and the accumulation of sufficient credits additionally earned (Scheme I); The other one is based on the successful completion of an NIAD-QE-approved program being provided by an educational institution that has been established legally, yet operates under

Table 1. All disciplinary fields in the degree-awarding by NIAD-QE in 2022

Literature	Commerce	Nutrition
Education	Business Administration	Engineering
Theology	Science	Design
Sociology	Pharmaceutical Sciences	Mercantile Marine Science
Liberal Arts	Nursing	Agriculture
Social Sciences	Health Science	Fisheries
Law	Acupuncture and Moxibustion	Home Economics
Political Science	Oral Health Science	Art
Economics	Judo Therapy	Physical Education

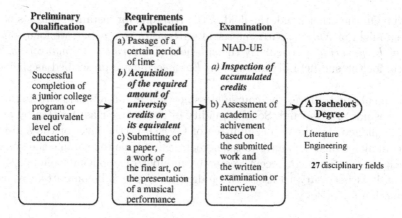

Fig. 1. Scheme for awarding degrees based on credit accumulation (Scheme I).

Table 2. Criteria for the *Information Engineering* sub-field.

Item 1	information engineering basic theory (4+ credits)
Item 2	computer system (4+ credits)
Item 3	information processing (4+ credits)
Item 4	relevant to information
Item 5	exercise and experiment about information engineering
Item 6	related course (4+ credits)
Item 7	others

the jurisdiction of ministries other than MEXT (Scheme II). While a Bachelor's degree can be earned under either of these two schemes, Masters and Doctoral degrees are awarded only under Scheme II. In this paper, we focus on the evaluation process in Scheme I. Figure 1 shows the procedures of application and evaluation for awarding degrees under Scheme I.

Although there exist similar systems as Scheme II in some other countries, the Scheme I of NIAD-QE is a unique system in the world [9,10,12,13]. To assist applicants, NIAD-QE annually publishes the application guidebook for Scheme I. In this paper we refer the 2022 version of it. In 2022, Bachelor's degrees are awarded in 27 disciplinary fields, as shown in Table 1.

An applicant has to demonstrate that he/she has accumulated the appropriate number of credits according to the criteria which are determined in each discipline. Some disciplinary fields are divided into sub-fields. When the field consists of two or more sub-fields, separate credit requirements are specified in each sub-field. Otherwise, the field itself may be considered a sub-field. For example, the *Engineering* field has nine sub-fields as follows: *Mechanical Engineering, Electrical and Electronics Engineering, Information Engineering, Applied Chemistry, Biological Technology, Materials Engineering, Civil Engineering, Architecture, Social Systems Engineering*. Each of these nine fields have its own set of criteria. On the other hand, the field of the *Nursing*, for instance, consists of the only sub-field of *Nursing* with one set of criteria. In this paper, we focus on the field of *Engineering*, particularly the sub-field of *Information Engineering*. The criteria for the sub-field of *Information Engineering* are prescribed as shown in Table 2.

As mentioned above, the course classification by an applicant to fulfill the criteria is not always valid. So, the validity of the course classification by applicants is judged, by the sub-committee of CVED, at the level of the sub-field. Sub-committee members have to take great deal of time to examine the syllabus of each course. Through recent years the number of applicants remains high, so that it is necessary to assist the judgment of the sub-committee by using information technology.

3   The Course-Classification-Support System Using the Deep Learning

3.1   Preparation of Training Data and Previous Methods

In 2002, using the Internet, Miyazaki et al. [6] collected 962 syllabi of the courses related to the *Information Engineering* curriculum offered by 13 universities in Japan. They read these syllabi and classified into the items listed in Table 3.

Table 3. Results of the manual classification.

Item	1	2	3	4	5	6	7
No. of syllabi	108	104	85	54	86	351	48

The papaers [6,7] proposed CCS and ACCS using these data. These systems are of traditional morphological analysis-based methods. It is therefore necessary to perform appropriate pre-processing such as data cleaning in advance, which places a heavy burden on the user.

On the other hand, in this paper, we construct a deep learning system using the syllabus of Items 1 to 6 as training data. It is assumable that one syllabus is related to multiple items. We, therefore, consider formulating the system to process multi-label problems to allow one syllabus to belong to multiple items.

3.2   Relationship with Related Works and Our Approach

The tasks dealt with in this paper require natural language processing. In particular, the problem dealt with in this paper can be regarded as a text classification problem. Various methods such as support vector machines (SVMs) have been proposed to solve classification problems in the machine learning field. Deep learning among them has been attracting attention in recent years, and there are increasing number of researches. Though deep learning is known to be powerful for image classification [3] and game problems [4,8], it has been applied to many classification problems that require natural language processing lately.

The natural language processing technology has made remarkable progress in recent years with the development of distributed representation technologies, such as word2vec [5]. In general, when deep learning is applied to natural language processing, the problem is how to configure the input to the network. There are cases where a sentence is divided into word units and the output value of word2vec is used as the input of the network. On the other hand, we use a more general technique called the Character-level CNN (CLCNN) [17].

With this method, the text is divided into character units, each of which is converted to a character code (e.g., Unicode value) and inputted to the network. As a result, the whole text can be treated as an image. It becomes advantageous to be able to use the results of many research studies on image processing. CLCNNs have been used, for example, in Retty (https://retty.me) where a web service allows users to find good restaurants.

In recent years, transformer [14] have been attracting attention in the field of text processing. Transformer is basically a method of learning the degree of association between words. It cannot be therefore directly applied to CLCNN that processes character by character. It also should be noted that pre-processing such as data cleaning, which has been done in CCS and ACCS, is important, especially in Japanese language processing since learning is performed word by word. Furthermore, from the point of view of the classification problem, existing methods such as SVM can be used instead of CNN. We decided to use CLCNN, which has many achievements as a method of inputting natural language character by character, since the problem of how a computer recognizes natural language also exists in SVM.

3.3 Proposed Method

The network consists of four layers, those are an input layer, a convolution layer, a pooling layer, and a fully connected layer. The network structure is shown in Fig. 2. The batch size and the number of epochs are 100 and 100, respectively. The Unicode value (UTF-8) was used when each character is inputted into the network. The first 500 characters in each syllabus were inputted and the rest of them were deleted. To syllabi with less than 500 characters, 0s were added to make them reach 500. For the same input, convolution was performed using multiple kernel sizes. Here, the kernel size was set to a width of the dimension size of one character and the height of n characters. As the value of n, four kinds of n = 2,3,4,5 were used. Through this, we expect that the convolution results will be similar to those with an n-gram. After passing the convolution results with multiple kernels to the pooling layers, they are passed through a fully connected layer consisting of 64 units to finally obtain 4 outputs (items 1, 2, 3 and 4), corresponding to the presence or absence of each item. In this study, we performed a batch normalization and dropout (the rate is 0.5) processes on the output of the fully connected layer.

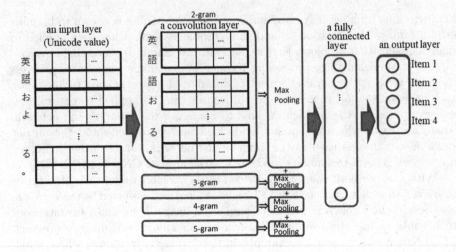

Fig. 2. Network structure.

4   Results and Discussion

Table 4 is the result of practice when the system was applied to the syllabus of courses provided in the field of *Information Engineering* at two national comprehensive universities: X University and Y University. The numbers of syllabi entered are 28 and 60, respectively. The tables show the number of syllabi that have been entered and then classified into the subject categories. In particular, the results of subject items 1 to 4 that are emphasized by the sub-committee are shown. The experiment was performed 10 times from No.1 to 10.

Although there were some variations in each experiment, it was confirmed that the results were close to those of the ACCS. ACCS has a high load of pre-processing such as data cleaning as already mentioned. It is therefore significant that CLCNN, which does not require such pre-processing, obtained results comparable to ACCS. In particular, we are considering application in actual sub-committee of CVED. The fact that the pre-processing can be reduced by deep learning is particularly important in actual operation, since now it takes a lot of preliminary work to carry out detailed preprocessing for all sub-fields.

In addition, when planning the application, it is important to shorten the actual work time. Essentially, our support system should be evaluated by comparing the work time with and without the use of it. But it is impossible to create an environment of accurate comparisons in practice of validation. We, therefore, compared the extent of reduction in the number of courses to be judged. In that sense as well, it is of great significance that we obtained results comparable to ACCS, which has already been confirmed to be more effective than CCS in terms of reducing the number of courses to be validated.

Table 4. Results of X and Y Universities.

No	X University					Y University				
	Item 1	Item 2	Item 3	Item 4	(Total)	Item 1	Item 2	Item 3	Item 4	(Total)
1	9	8	4	13	34	27	24	12	29	92
2	10	17	4	12	43	44	18	17	43	122
3	11	8	3	10	32	44	30	21	38	133
4	9	14	3	10	36	25	25	17	50	117
5	9	8	4	18	39	20	20	20	14	74
6	13	22	3	13	51	38	21	10	43	112
7	10	13	3	8	34	25	19	9	23	76
8	11	20	7	12	50	23	19	20	22	84
9	10	14	3	17	44	28	18	14	31	91
10	9	12	3	14	38	38	22	24	41	125
Average	10.1	13.6	3.7	12.7	40.1	21.2	21.6	16.4	33.4	103
ACCS	9	12	3	6	30	29	17	16	24	86

5   Conclusions

In this paper, we proposed a course-classification-support system using the deep learning. It was confirmed that the method using deep learning proposed in this paper can obtain the same level of performance as the conventionally promising ACCS.

We are planning to use this system in the actual practice of assessment by sub-committees to confirm its effectiveness in near future. It is necessarily to prepare training data first. The courses must be classified according to pre-determined criteria. The criteria are determined in each discipline. Some disciplinary fields are divided into sub-fields. It is therefore necessary to prepare a large amount of training data that will be the correct classification for each discipline and sub-fields. However, majority of syllabi published before 2010s are not degitalized but paper-based. It is a barrier when we prepare the training data. We have hired dedicated staff to digitize the syllabi, that is actually judged and whose categories are known in order to overcome this problem.

Furthermore, it is essential to cooperate with the *Degree Validation and Examination Division*, that is responsible for the examination of degrees at NIAD-QE. NIAD-QE awards thousands of degrees each year and have extensive data on those applicants. It takes a lot of effort to extract the data necessary for the course classification support system proposed in this paper. Therefore, it will be important to create a system while taking into consideration the linkage with the huge amout of data archived by the Degree Validation and Examination Division.

Acknoledgement. We would like to thank the staff of the Degree Validation and Examination Division for providing the data for this study.

References

1. Ida, M., Nozawa, T., Yoshikane, F., Miyazaki, K., Kita, H.: Development of syllabus database and its application to comparative analysis of curricula among majors in undergraduate education. Res. Acad. Degrees Univ. Eval. **2**, 85–96 (2005). (in Japanese)
2. Itoh, E., Matsunaga, Y., Yamada, S., Hirokawa, S.: Auto DB construction from Web syllabus. In: The 17th Annual Conference of the Japanese Society for Artificial Intelligence, 1D4-08 (2003). (in Japanese)
3. Le, Q.V.: building high-level features using large scale unsupervised learning. In: Proceedings of the 29th International Conference on Machine Learning, 507–514 (2012)
4. Mnih, V.: Playing Atari with deep reinforcement learning. In: NIPS Deep Learning Workshop 2013 (2013)
5. Mikolov, T., Chen, K., Corrado, G., Dean, J.: Efficient estimation of word representations in vector space. arXiv:1301.3781 (2013)
6. Miyazaki, K., Ida, M., Yoshikane, F., Nozawa, T., Kita, H.: On development of a course classification support system using syllabus data. Comput. Eng. I, 311–318 (2004)
7. Miyazaki, K., Ida, M., Yoshikane, F., Nozawa, T., Kita, H.: Proposal of the active course classification support system to support the classification of courses at the degree-awarding of NIAD-UE. In: Proceedings of 6th International Symposium on Advanced Intelligent Systems, pp. 685–690 (2005)
8. Miyazaki, K.: Exploitation-oriented learning with deep learning introducing profit sharing to a deep Q-network. J. Adv. Comput. Intell. Intelligent Inf. **21**(5), 849–855 (2017)
9. Mori, R.: System of assessment of learning outcomes in regents college: evaluation of learning and credit. Res. Acad. Degrees, **10**, 107–129 (1999). (in Japanese)
10. Mori, R.: The credit transfer system and the validation service at the open university. Res. Acad. Degrees, **17**, 183–198 (2003). (in Japanese)
11. Nozawa, T., Ida, M., Yoshikane, F., Miyazaki, K., Kita, H.: Construction of curriculum analyzing system based on document clustering of syllabus data. J. Inf. Process. **46**(1), 289–300 (2005). (in Japanese)
12. Puirseil, S., Quality assuarance in irish higher education - the higher education and training awards council. Res. Acad. Degrees **15**, 124–140 (2001)
13. Tachi, A.: A study on thomas edison state college, the external degree college established by the state of New Jersey. Res. Acad. Degrees **10**, 73–89 (1999). (in Japanese)
14. Vaswani, A., et al.: Attention is all you need. In: Neural Information Processing Systems (NIPS 2017) (2017)
15. Yamada, S., Itou, E., Hirokawa, S.: A study and analysis of auto collected web syllabus pages. Forum Inf. Technol. 2002 (FIT2002), **32**, 301–302 (2002). (in Japanese)
16. Yamada, S., Matsunaga, Y., Itou, E., Hirokawa, S.: A study of design for intelligent web syllabus crawling agent. Trans. IEICE. D-I, **86**(8), 566–574 (2003). (in Japanese)
17. Zhang, X, Zhao, J., LeCun, Y.: Characterlevel convolutional networks for text classification. arXiv:1509.01626 (2015)

A Research of Infectivity Rate of Seasonal Influenza from Pre-infectious Person for Data Driven Simulation

Saori Iwanaga(✉) ⓘ

Japan Coast Guard Academy, Kure, Hiroshima 737-8512, Japan
s-iwanaga@jcga.ac.jp

Abstract. I had proposed a discrete mathematical SEPIR (Susceptible – Exposed - Pre-infectious – Infectious - Recovered stage) model for seasonal influenza. In a subsequent previously study, focusing on infections by a pre-infectious person using pre-existing data, I showed that there super-spreading of seasonal influenza occurred before D-day that the first patients are discovered at Japan Coast Guard Academy. In this study, I found that the infectivity rate from pre-infectious people is 0.041 when the surrounding people don't take counter-measures against the infection. After D-day in the community, the countermeasures taken reduce the infectivity rate to 0.002 in working spaces and 0.013 in living spaces. And the number of infectious people can be estimated simply by the summing up each group in the community.

Keywords: Epidemic model · Seasonal influenza · Super-spread · Infectivity rate

1 Introduction

The US Centers for Disease Control and Prevention (CDC) [1] has reported that the symptoms of seasonal influenza, what is called flu, arise within one to four days after the virus enters the body. Thus, a person can transmit it to others before they know that they are sick, as well as while they are sick. In other words, flu has an incubation period. Moreover, it has two periods, the exposed period and the infectious period, but neither have any symptoms at this stage.

By retrospective investigation of activities in closed spaces used by the students using epidemic data, we just have to deal with dormitories and classrooms as closed spaces for infection channels [2]. Then, almost all infections were transmitted on campus. For this investigation, a refinement was introduced to a previous epidemic model to account for the incubation period and proposed a discrete-time SEPIR (Susceptible – Exposed - Pre-infectious – Infectious - Recovered) model for flu. In this manner, I derived an incubation period of three days from epidemic data and showed that students can infect others beginning two day before symptoms show [2].

Focusing on the infectivity rate, simulation of a flu epidemic using the SEPIR model with a multi-agent simulation and a real spatio-temporal model was performed [3]. To

Y. Kambayashi et al. (Eds.): AICON 2022, LNICST 477, pp. 131–143, 2023.
https://doi.org/10.1007/978-3-031-29126-5_11

perform a realistic simulation, the infectivity rate from epidemic data was calculated. This simulation of the epidemic with various infectivity rates calculated by the average for the whole academy, for type of rooms, for each year, for double lessons and for multi-year classes were compared. However, the simulation results are very different from the epidemic data and the peak of the simulated epidemic is higher than the real one. Infection in classroom is a key point because the number of students in classroom is more than that of dormitories.

By retrospective investigation of all infected students at the pre-infectious stage, but have no symptoms, some students super-spread flu until the day that first patients are discovered, which is defined D-day. After D-day, a few students were infected [4]. Students were directed to start wearing masks, washing hands and better ventilating rooms, amongst other measures, when flu is first discovered. After D-day, the measures seem to take effect after about one day and the infectivity rate become lower.

2 Proposed SEPIR Model

Traditional epidemic mathematical model is SIR model [5], and the state transition diagram of an individual is shown in Fig. 1(a). Keeling et al. [6] deal with incubation period and propose mathematical SEIR model which many childhood infectious diseases (such as measles, rubella, or chickenpox) follow. The state transition diagram of an individual is shown in Fig. 1(b). In those models, only an infected "I" individual can infect a susceptible "S" individual.

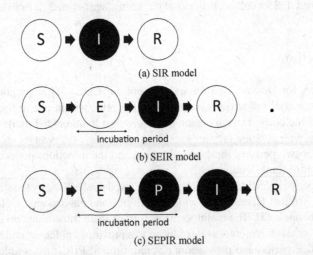

(a) SIR model

(b) SEIR model

(c) SEPIR model

Fig. 1. The state transition diagram of an infected individual: the circles show the state of individual. S: Susceptible state, E: Exposed state, P: Pre-infectious state, I: Infectious state and R: Recovered state. The black circle mean that they can affect others.

The pre-infectious state "P", that is asymptomatic was introduced into the SEIR model and proposed the discrete mathematical SEPIR model for flu [2]. The incubation period is divided into two periods, the exposed period and the infectious period, with neither having any symptoms. The former was set as the exposed state "E" and the latter as the pre-infectious state "P". The state transition diagram is shown in Fig. 1(c).

An individual of "I" or "P" can infect a "S" individual. The probability of contact between individuals of susceptible "S" and infectious "I" is determined by their respective numbers. Considering a mean infectivity rate β, an individual of "S" moves to exposed "E", which is shown in Eq. (1) [5]. The probability of contact between individuals of "S" and "P" is also determined by their respective numbers. By introducing infectivity rate α, an individual of "S" moves to "E" as given in Eq. (1) [2]. By introducing transmission rate σ, an individual of "E" moves to "P" as given in Eq. (2) [2]. By introducing transmission rate τ, an individual of "P" moves to "I" as given in Eq. (3) [2]. By introducing recovery rate γ which is the inverse of the infectious "I" period, this leads to a far more straightforward equation as shown in Eq. (4) [5]. Here, S(t), E(t), P(t), I(t) and R(t) is the number of individuals of "S", "E", "P", "I" and "R", t representing day.

$$\Delta S = S(t+1) - S(t) = -\alpha S(t)P(t) - \beta S(t)I(t) \tag{1}$$

$$\Delta E = E(t+1) - E(t) = \alpha S(t)P(t) + \beta S(t)I(t) - \sigma E(t) \tag{2}$$

$$\Delta P = P(t+1) - P(t) = \sigma E(t) - \tau P(t) \tag{3}$$

$$\Delta I = I(t+1) - I(t) = \tau P(t) - \gamma I(t) \tag{4}$$

$$\Delta R = R(t+1) - R(t) = \gamma I(t) \tag{5}$$

3 Epidemic Situations

3.1 Situation A

In January, 2017, an epidemic of flu occurred at the Japan Coast Guard Academy (JCGA). JCGA is a residential college. At that time, there were 150 undergraduate students, consisting of 56 freshmen, 47 sophomores, 44 juniors and just 3 seniors due to the others being on away for on ship training. After a three-day holiday from January 7th to 9th, students returned to their dormitories and resumed to take classes. On Friday January 13th, two students, a freshman and a sophomore, showed symptoms of flu. 37 students, that is 20 freshmen, 13 sophomores and 4 juniors, showed symptoms in the next two weeks.

3.2 Situation B

In January, 2019, an epidemic of flu also occurred on the JCGA training ship. After winter vacation until January 3rd, students returned to the academy and started embarkation training. On Friday January 10th, one student showed signs of flu. Within two weeks there were 18 cases out of 56 freshmen.

3.3 Situation C

In January, 2019, a separate flu epidemic occurred at JCGA. At that time, there were
109 undergraduate students excluding freshmen[1] (54 sophomores, 51 juniors and just
4 seniors) as the others were conducting on board training. After the winter vacation
until January 3rd, students returned to the dormitories and resumed to take classes. On
Thursday January 9th, six students exhibited flu. 13 students, that is 11 sophomores and
2 juniors, showed symptoms within two weeks.

4 Parameters

4.1 Infectivity Rate

We adopted SIR model and input our academy's data. The estimated parameters are $\beta =$
0.0014 per day (normalized $\beta = 0.21$) and $1/\gamma = 4.0$ days in situation A using a simple
squares method. And the basic reproductive ratio R0, which is determined by normalized
$\beta/\gamma = 0.83$. The initial results [2] were found to be incorrect so were recalculated. These
results were then found to be out of range for human's influenza, between 3 and 4 [5].
In situation B, estimated parameters are $\beta = 0.0034$ per day (normalized $\beta = 0.19$) and
$1/\gamma = 4.5$ days, given an R0 of 0.85. In situation C, estimated parameters are $\beta = 0.0008$
per day (normalized $\beta = 0.045$) and $1/\gamma = 6.7$ days, given an R0 of 0.30. Situation B
and C are also out of range of human influenza. According to the parameter β and SIR
model, no one was infected in situation A, B and C. Then, SIR model doesn't match
JCGA situations.

At JCGA, though patients are isolated in sick rooms, a flu epidemic occurred. It
is assumed that pre-infectious students infected others. The infectivity rate β by "I" in
Eq. (1) is set as 0. Students had already infected many students until the day of the first
patients being discovered, which is defined as D-day. I calculated the infectivity rate
α from "P" of situation A and B in the classrooms and dormitories before D-day and
after D-day using epidemic data in Table 1, where cases of super-spreading occurred
[4]. In Table 1, the average, the standard deviation, maximum value and minimum value
of the infectivity rate are shown. I found that the average infectivity rate (α_bC) before
D-day in situation A and B is about 0.04. And the average infectivity rate (α_aC) after
D-day is smaller than that before D-day. It seems that the countermeasures against flu
after D-day were effective. N refers to the number of infections. Infection occurred a
few times in situation B. In situation C, the average infectivity rate was small, where
super-spreading didn't occurred.

Table 2 shows the infectivity rate in the dormitories in all of situations A, B and C.
The average infectivity rate (α_bB) before D-day in situation A and B was about 0.04.
And the average infectivity rate (α_aC) after D-day was smaller than that before. It seems
that the countermeasures against flu after D-day were effective. Infections occurred a
few times in situation B. The average infectivity rate in situation C was very small and
infection occurred a few times, as super-spreading didn't occur.

---

[1] In January 2019 the freshmen had no contacts with other students and were trained by different
staff.

In situation A and B, where super-spreading occurred, the total average infectivity rates before D-day was about 0.041 as shown in Table 3. This shows that two "S" students were infected and become "E" the next day if there was a "P" student in the room of 50. The infectivity rate in the classrooms and dormitories after D-day are small. This suggests that students are more infectious before D-day than after. And the total average infectivity rate (α_aC) in the classrooms after D-day is 0.002 and that in dormitories 0.013. This suggests that students in the dormitories are seven times more infectious than in the classrooms. That is, after D-day, the infectivity rate must be calculated for type of rooms.

Table 1. Infectivity rate in classrooms.

Infectivity rate	situation A		situation B		situation C
	α_bC	α_aC	α_bC	α_aC	α_C
The average	0.0423	0.0019	0.0431	0.0008	0.0021
Standard deviation	0.0886	0.0049	0.0192	0.0015	0.0017
Max	0.3200	0.0185	0.0648	0.0038	0.0035
Min	0	0	0.0182	0	0
N	25	29	3	5	5

Table 2. Infectivity rate in dormitories.

Infectivity rate	situation A		situation B		situation C
	α_bB	α_aB	α_bB	α_aB	α_B
The average	0.0391	0.0152	0.0373	0.0014	0.0068
Standard deviation	0.0853	0.0430	0.0105	0.0030	0.0304
Max	0.2857	0.1667	0.0500	0.0082	0.1429
Min	0	0	0.0244	0	0
N	21	34	3	6	21

Comparing all situations, super-spreading didn't occur in situation C, which is the situation where infections occurred a very few times in the classrooms compared with the dormitories. In situation C, infection times is very small in the classrooms for all days compared with situation A. This fact is considered to be the reason why super-spreading didn't occur. In other words, super-spreading is more likely to occur in the classrooms.

Table 3. The total average infectivity rate in situation A and B.

Infectivity rate	By D-day		After D-day	
	classrooms	dormitory	classrooms	dormitory
	α_bC	α_bB	α_aB	α_aB
The average	0.041		0.002	0.013

4.2 The Number of Susceptible Students

In a former study, I investigated multi-layer activities, such as in the classrooms, study rooms or dormitories. In situation A, it is estimated that 16 students were infected in the classrooms, one in the dormitories and five in one of the two locations on weekdays [2]. That is, the majority of the students were infected in the classrooms. The number of infected students relates to the number of "S" students.

In situation A, the number of infected students in the classrooms before D-day was 19 (excluding the lecture hall where all students attended) and that after is two as shown in Table 4. In the dormitories, that in the classrooms before D-day was six and that after is four. Many students were infected before D-day in classrooms.

The average number of susceptible "S" students in the classrooms before D-day was 33 (excluding the lecture hall where all students attended) and that after is 50. And that in the classrooms before D-day was 7.3 that after is 6.8. That is, I found that students were infected even in small classrooms before D-day.

Table 4. The number of infected students in situation A.

	In classrooms		In dormitories	
	Before D-day	After D-day	Before D-day	After D-day
Infected students	19	2	6	4
Average number of "S"	33.0	50.0	7.3	6.8

5 Near Decomposability

5.1 Definition

On theoretical grounds, Simon shows the following [7]. Hierarchic system has a property, near decomposability, that is interactions within each subsystem are stronger than the interaction among subsystems. For example, in an organization, there will generally be more interaction within employees who belong to the same department than among employees from different departments. In organic substances intermolecular forces will generally be weaker than molecular forces, and molecular forces weaker than nuclear forces. Then, we can distinguish between the interactions among subsystems and the interactions within subsystems and that simplifies the behavior. Here, the former is set as contact network in the bedrooms and the latter is set as contact network in the classrooms.

According to Eq. (1), the number of infected students relates to the number of the students in the rooms because the infectivity rates before D-day were almost same in the classrooms and dormitories. And 20 cases out of 26 were campus transmissions before D-day [4]. D-day is January 13th in situation A.

In this study, I adopt near decomposability to JCGA situations and I roughly estimate the epidemic. Focusing on classrooms, I subdivided situation A [4] into school year as shown in Table 5. Rows G1, G2 and G3 refer receptivity to the daily number of infected freshmen, senior and junior students by pre-infectious "P" students in the classrooms. The dates underlined refer to days off. According to a former study, super-spreading (SS) is defined that when people directly infected more than 6.7% of people in their community in one day [4]. The threshold of SS in italics are shown in Table 5, which is 3.7 of 56 freshmen, 3.1 of 47 sophomores, 2.9 of 44 juniors. I found that SS occurred in the classrooms of freshmen on January 11th, which is shown in bold. It is almost SS in the classrooms of sophomores on January 11th.

Table 5. Epidemic of flu at JCGA in January, 2017 (situation A) divided by school year.

	9	10	11	12	13	14	15	16	17	18	19	20	21	22	23	24	25	26	SS
G1			10	3	0	1	0	0	1	0	0	0							3.7
G2			3	2	0	2	0	1	0	0	0								3.1
G3				1	1	1	0	0	0										2.9

5.2 Rough Estimation

Table 6 is the rough estimation of infection for each school year. For freshmen, the epidemic data of students 1, 4, 7, 17 and 35 are used, and it is assumed that student 1 infected 51 freshmen in the classrooms.

There are no "P" students before January 10th. On January 11th, the number of S and P in freshmen's classrooms were 51 and 1, ΔS is -2 ($= -0.041 * 51 * 1$) using Eq. (1). That is, two students (A1, A2) were exposed and changed "E" from "S" the next day. On January 12th, the number of S and P in the classrooms was 49 and 1, two students (B1, B2) were exposed. The number of S and P in the classrooms was 47 and 2 on January 13th, four students (C1–C4) were exposed. There were no classes on that weekend. The number of S and P on January 16th in the classrooms were 43 and 4, ΔS is 0 ($= -0.002 * 43 * 4$) and no one got infected. Then, 8 freshmen were estimated to be infected in the classrooms. Similarly, the epidemic data of students 2, 3, 5, 6 and 31 are used and it is assumed that student 2 infected 42 sophomores in the sophomore's classrooms as shown in Table 7.

Table 6. Rough estimate for freshmen (56 students) in situation A

ID	D	Date																	
		9	10	11	12	13	14	15	16	17	18	19	20	21	22	23	24	25	26
1	1	S	E	P	P	I	I	I	I	R	R	R	R	R	R	R	R	R	R·
A1	1	S	S	S	E	P	P	I	I	I	I	R	R	R	R	R	R	R	R
A2	1·	S	S	S	E	P	P	I	I	I	I	R	R	R	R	R	R	R	R
B1	1	S	S	S	S	E	P	P	I	I	I	R	R	R	R	R	R	R	R
B2	1	S	S	S	S	E	P	P	I	I	I	R	R	R	R	R	R	R	R
C1	1	S	S	S	S	S	E	P	P	I	I	I	R	R	R	R	R	R	R
C2	1	S	S	S	S	S	E	P	P	I	I	I	R	R	R	R	R	R	R
C3	1	S	S	S	S	S	E	P	P	I	I	I	R	R	R	R	R	R	R
C4	1	S	S	S	S	S	E	P	P	I	I	I	I	R	R	R	R	R	R
	S	52	51	51	49	47	43	43	43	43	43	43	43	43	43	43	43	43	43
	E	0	1	0	2	2	4	0	0	0	0	0	0	0	0	0	0	0	0
	P	0	0	1	1	2	4	6	4	0	0	0	0	0	0	0	0	0	0
	I	0	0	0	0	1	1	3	5	8	8	4	1	0	0	0	0	0	0
	R	0	0	0	0	0	0	0	0	1	1	5	8	9	9	9	9	9	9
	ΔS	0	0	-2	-2	-4	0	0	0	0	0	0	0	0	0	0	0	0	0
4	1	S	S	E	P	P	I	I	I	I	I	R	R	R	R	R	R	R	R
7	1	S	S	E	P	P	I	I	I	R	R	R	R	R	R	R	R	R	R
17	1	S	S	S	E	P	P	I	I	I	I	R	R	R	R	R	R	R	R
35	1	S	S	S	S	S	S	S	E	P	P	I	I	I	I	R	R	R	R

As for situation B, the epidemic data of students 1, 2, and 18 are used and it is assumed that student 1 and 2 infected 53 freshmen in the classrooms as shown Table 8. D-day is January 10th in situation B. There are no "P" students before January 7th. On January 8th, the number of S and P in freshmen's classrooms were 53 and 1, ΔS is -2 ($= -0.041 * 53 * 1$) using Eq. (1). That is, two students (G1, G2) were infected and changed "E" from "S" the next day. The number of S and P on January 9th in the classrooms were 51 and 2, four students (H1–H4) were infected. The number of S and P on January 10th in the classrooms were 47 and 3, six students (I1–I6) were infected. The number of S and P on January 11th in the classrooms were 41 and 6, ΔS is 0 ($= -0.002 * 41 * 6$) and no one got infected. There are no classes on that weekend. Then, 12 freshmen are estimated to be infected in the classrooms.

Table 7. Rough estimation for sophomores (47 students) in situation A

ID	D	Date																	
		9	10	11	12	13	14	15	16	17	18	19	20	21	22	23	24	25	26
2	2	S	E	P	P	I	I	I	I	R	R	R	R	R	R	R	R	R	R
D1	2	S	S	S	E	P	P	I	I	I	I	R	R	R	R	R	R	R	R
D2	2	S	S	S	E	P	P	I	I	I	I	R	R	R	R	R	R	R	R
E1	2	S	S	S	S	E	P	P	I	I	I	I	R	R	R	R	R	R	R
E2	2	S	S	S	S	E	P	P	I	I	I	I	R	R	R	R	R	R	R
F1	2	S	S	S	S	S	E	P	P	I	I	I	I	R	R	R	R	R	R
F2	2	S	S	S	S	S	E	P	P	I	I	I	I	R	R	R	R	R	R
F3	2	S	S	S	S	S	E	P	P	I	I	I	I	R	R	R	R	R	R
	S	43	42	42	40	38	35	35	35	35	35	35	35	35	35	35	35	35	35
	E	0	1	0	2	2	3	0	0	0	0	0	0	0	0	0	0	0	0
	P	0	0	1	1	2	4	5	3	0	0	0	0	0	0	0	0	0	0
	I	0	0	0	0	1	1	3	5	7	7	5	3	0	0	0	0	0	0
	R	0	0	0	0	0	0	0	0	1	1	3	5	8	8	8	8	8	8
	ΔS	0	0	−2	−2	−3	0	0	0	0	0	0	0	0	0	0	0	0	0
3	2	S	S	E	P	P	I	I	I	I	I	R	R	R	R	R	R	R	R
5	2	S	S	E	P	P	I	I	I	I	I	R	R	R	R	R	R	R	R
6	2	S	S	E	P	P	I	I	I	I	R	R	R	R	R	R	R	R	R
31	2	S	S	S	S	S	S	E	P	P	I	I	I	I	R	R	R	R	R

As for situation C, the epidemic data of students from 1 to 10 and 12 are used and it is assumed that students from 1 to 6 students infected 43 sophomores in the classrooms as shown Table 9. Here, super-spreading didn't occurred and the infectivity rate is set as 0.002. 2 sophomores are estimated to be infected in the classrooms.

On January 7th, the number of S and P in sophomores' classrooms were 43 and 6, ΔS is -1 ($= -0.002 * 43 * 6$) using Eq. (1). That is, one student (J1) was infected. The number of S and P on January 8h in the classrooms were 42 and 6, one student (K1) was infected.

Table 8. Rough estimation for freshmen (56 students) in situation B

ID	D	4	5	6	7	8	9	10	11	12	13	14	15	16	17
								D	**a**	**t**	**e**				
1	1	S	S	S	E	P	P	I	I	I	I	I	I	R	R
2	1	S	S	S	S	E	P	P	I	I	I	I	I	R	R
G1	1	S	S	S	S	S	E	P	P	I	I	I	I	R	R
G2	1	S	S	S	S	S	E	P	P	I	I	I	I	R	R
H1	1	S	S	S	S	S	S	E	P	P	I	I	I	I	R
H2	1	S	S	S	S	S	S	E	P	P	I	I	I	I	R
H3	1	S	S	S	S	S	S	E	P	P	I	I	I	I	R
H4	1	S	S	S	S	S	S	E	P	P	I	I	I	I	R
I1	1	S	S	S	S	S	S	S	E	P	P	I	I	I	I
I2	1	S	S	S	S	S	S	S	E	P	P	I	I	I	I
I3	1	S	S	S	S	S	S	S	E	P	P	I	I	I	I
I4	1	S	S	S	S	S	S	S	E	P	P	I	I	I	I
I5	1	S	S	S	S	S	S	S	E	P	P	I	I	I	I
I6	1	S	S	S	S	S	S	S	E	P	P	I	I	I	I
S		55	55	55	54	53	51	47	41	41	41	41	41	41	41
E		0	0	0	1	1	2	4	6	0	0	0	0	0	0
P		0	0	0	0	1	2	3	6	10	6	0	0	0	0
I		0	0	0	0	0	0	1	2	4	8	14	14	10	6
R		0	0	0	0	0	0	0	0	0	0	0	0	4	8
ΔS		0	0	0	0	-2	-4	-6	0	0	0	0	0	0	0
18	1	S	S	S	S	S	S	S	S	S	S	S	S	S	S

ID	D	18	19	20	21	22	23	24	25	26	27	28	29	30
cont.							**D**	**a**	**t**	**e**				
1	1	R	R	R	R	R	R	R	R	R	R	R	R	R
2	1	R	R	R	R	R	R	R	R	R	R	R	R	R
G1	1	R	R	R	R	R	R	R	R	R	R	R	R	R
G2	1	R	R	R	R	R	R	R	R	R	R	R	R	R
H1	1	R	R	R	R	R	R	R	R	R	R	R	R	R
H2	1	R	R	R	R	R	R	R	R	R	R	R	R	R
H3	1	R	R	R	R	R	R	R	R	R	R	R	R	R
H4	1	R	R	R	R	R	R	R	R	R	R	R	R	R
I1	1	R	R	R	R	R	R	R	R	R	R	R	R	R
I2	1	R	R	R	R	R	R	R	R	R	R	R	R	R
I3	1	R	R	R	R	R	R	R	R	R	R	R	R	R
I4	1	R	R	R	R	R	R	R	R	R	R	R	R	R
I5	1	R	R	R	R	R	R	R	R	R	R	R	R	R
I6	1	R	R	R	R	R	R	R	R	R	R	R	R	R
S		41	41	41	41	41	41	41	41	41	41	41	41	41
E		0	0	0	0	0	0	0	0	0	0	0	0	0
P		0	0	0	0	0	0	0	0	0	0	0	0	0
I		0	0	0	0	0	0	0	0	0	0	0	0	0
R		14	14	14	14	14	14	14	14	14	14	14	14	14
ΔS		0	0	0	0	0	0	0	0	0	0	0	0	0
18	1	S	E	P	P	I	I	I	I	I	I	R	R	R

Table 9. Rough estimation for sophomores (54 students) in situation C

ID	D	4	5	6	7	8	9	10	11	12	13	14	15	16	17
								D	a	t	e				
1	1	S	S	E	P	P	I	I	I	I	I	I	R	R	R
2	1	S	S	E	P	P	I	I	I	I	I	I	R	R	R
3	1	S	S	E	P	P	I	I	I	I	I	I	R	R	R
4	1	S	S	E	P	P	I	I	I	I	I	I	R	R	R
5	1	S	S	E	P	P	I	I	I	I	I	I	R	R	R
6	1	S	S	E	P	P	I	I	I	I	I	I	R	R	R
J1	1	S	S	S	S	E	P	P	I	I	I	I	R	R	R
K1	1	S	S	S	S	S	E	P	P	I	I	I	I	R	R
	S	49	49	43	43	42	41	41	41	41	41	41	41	41	41
	E	0	0	6	0	1	1	0	0	0	0	0	0	0	0
	P	0	0	0	6	6	1	2	1	0	0	0	0	0	0
	I	0	0	0	0	0	6	6	7	8	8	8	1	0	0
	R	0	0	0	0	0	0	0	0	0	0	0	·7	8	8
	ΔS	0	0	0	-1	-1	0	0	0	0	0	0	0	0	0
7	2	S	S	S	E	P	P	I	I	I	I	I	I	R	R
8	2	S	S	S	E	P	P	I	I	I	I	I	I	R	R
9	2	S	S	S	E	P	P	I	I	I	I	I	R	R	R
10	2	S	S	S	S	E	P	P	I	I	I	I	I	I	R
12	2	S	S	S	S	S	S	S	E	P	P	I	I	I	

ID	D	18	19	20	21	22	23	24	25	26	27	28	29	30
cont.								D	a	t	e			
1	2	R	R	R	R	R	R	R	R	R	R	R	R	R
2	2	R	R	R	R	R	R	R	R	R	R	R	R	R
3	2	R	R	R	R	R	R	R	R	R	R	R	R	R
4	2	R	R	R	R	R	R	R	R	R	R	R	R	R
5	2	R	R	R	R	R	R	R	R	R	R	R	R	R
6	2	R	R	R	R	R	R	R	R	R	R	R	R	R
J1	2	R	R	R	R	R	R	R	R	R	R	R	R	R
K1	2	R	R	R	R	R	R	R	R	R	R	R	R	R
	S	41	41	41	41	41	41	41	41	41	41	41	41	41
	E	0	0	0	0	0	0	0	0	0	0	0	0	0
	P	0	0	0	0	0	0	0	0	0	0	0	0	0
	I	0	0	0	0	0	0	0	0	0	0	0	0	0
	R	8	8	8	8	8	8	8	8	8	8	8	8	8
	ΔS	0	0	0	0	0	0	0	0	0	0	0	0	0
7	2	R	R	R	R	R	R	R	R	R	R	R	R	R
8	2	R	R	R	R	R	R	R	R	R	R	R	R	R
9	2	R	R	R	R	R	R	R	R	R	R	R	R	R
10	2	R	R	R	R	R	R	R	R	R	R	R	R	R
12	2	I	I	I	R	R	R	R	R	R	R	R	R	R

6 Discussion

Figure 2(a) shows a rough estimation of infections in situation A. Compared with the epidemic data, the rough estimation looks low because it is assumed that students have one class in a day. In fact, freshmen had four classes on January 11th and two classes on January 12th (from epidemic data) [2]. Figure 2(b) is the transmission of rough estimation of situation B. Compared with the epidemic data, the rough estimation looks little low as well. Figure 2(c) is the transmission of rough estimation of situation C. Compared with the epidemic data, the rough estimation looks little low as well. Sophomores had four classes on January 7th and three classes on January 8th (from epidemic data).

Here, on January 12th in 2017, there was a lecture for all 150 students. The number of S and P was 129 and 7, ΔS is -37 ($= -0.041 * 129 * 7$) using Eq. (1). That is, 37 students got infected and changed "E" from "S" the next day. Super-spreading might be expected but it didn't occur as seats were set separately for each school year. It is similar to the summing up for each school year.

I could roughly estimate the epidemic by near decomposability, that is I subdivided the situations into school years. This shows that it is a key point to prevent the contact of many people in closed spaces such as classrooms as a counter-measure against flu.

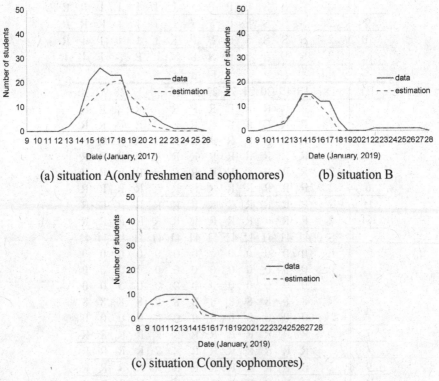

(a) situation A(only freshmen and sophomores)   (b) situation B

(c) situation C(only sophomores)

Fig. 2. Rough estimation of infections

7   Conclusion

By examining infections by a pre-infectious person using pre-existing data at JCGA, I found that the infectivity rate from pre-infectious people is 0.041 when the surrounding people don't take counter-measures against the infection. After D-day the first patients are discovered in the community, the countermeasures taken reduced the infectivity rate to 0.002 in working spaces and 0.013 in living spaces. And the number of infectious people can be estimated simply by the summing up each group in the community.

References

1. CDC spread. https://www.cdc.gov/flu/about/disease/spread.htm
2. Iwanaga, S., Kawaguchi, K.: Analysis of epidemic of Seasonal Influenza closed space. In: Proceedings of the 22nd Asia Pacific Symposium on Intelligent and Evolutionary Systems, pp. 37–44 (2018)
3. Iwanaga, S., Yoshida, H., Kinjo, S.: Feasibility study on multi-agent simulations of a seasonal influenza epidemic in a closed space. In: Sato, H., Iwanaga, S., Ishii, A. (eds.) Proceedings of the 23rd Asia Pacific Symposium on Intelligent and Evolutionary Systems, pp. 203–215. Springer, Cham (2020). https://doi.org/10.1007/978-3-030-37442-6_19
4. Iwanaga, S.: Super-spreading is possible by the day the first patients are discovered in the community. J. Adv. Artif. Life Robot. 3(1), 24–31 (2022)
5. Kermack, W.O., McKendrick, A.G.: A contribution to the mathematical theory of epidemics. Proc. R. Soc. Lond. Ser. A 115(772), 700–721 (1927)
6. Keeling, M.J., Rohani, P.: Modeling Infectious Diseases in Humans and Animals. Princeton University Press (2008)
7. Simon, H.A.: The Sciences of the Artificial. The MIT Press (1996)

Creating Trust Within Population of Evolutionary Computation in an Uncertain Environment Using Blockchain

Hiroshi Sato[(✉)] and Masao Kubo

National Defense Academy of Japan, Yokosuka, Kanagawa 239-8686, Japan
hsato@nda.ac.jp

Abstract. Various population-based optimization methods have been proposed following the development of evolutionary computation. Optimization is achieved through the interactions of many individuals in these systems. However, reliability becomes an issue when the system is implemented in a distributed environment. It may not be possible to trust others in such an environment. Many factors, such as malfunction of distributed parts or failure to synchronize, will break the trust. Therefore, there must be some mechanism that can build trust between distributed individuals. The record of past actions is usually a good source for trust building. This paper utilizes the blockchain mechanism for the population-based optimization system to make a trust management system. By using blockchain, we can implement trust without a central authority. In the system, all interactions are reviewed and get feedback, and the feedback is used to calculate the trust score.

Keywords: Trusted system · Blockchain · Surrogate Assisted Evolutionary Computation

1 Introduction

Numerous population-based optimization methods have been devised since the 1950s. For example, Genetic Algorithm [1], Genetic Programming [2], Evolutionary Strategies [3], and Evolutionary Programming [4] are the pioneers in this field. Following the success of evolutionary computation, a lot of other population-based algorithms have been devised, such as Particle Swarm Optimization [5], Ant Colony Optimization [6], and Artificial Immune Systems [7]. In these systems, optimization is achieved through the interactions of many solution candidates. They are called individuals, particles, or agents. In this paper, we use the word "individuals" to refer to a solution candidate.

Reliability becomes an issue when the system is implemented in a distributed computational environment. In such an environment, it may not be possible to trust others such as Byzantine generals problem [8]. There are many cases in which we cannot guarantee trust in individuals, such as malfunction of distributed components, failure to synchronize the information, or injection of

Y. Kambayashi et al. (Eds.): AICON 2022, LNICST 477, pp. 144–150, 2023.
https://doi.org/10.1007/978-3-031-29126-5_12

malicious individuals. Therefore, there must be some mechanism that can build trust between distributed individuals. In these cases, the record of past actions is usually a good tool for generating trust.

Moreover, the fitness information will be vague even in a single machine when the system uses a surrogate mechanism [9]. Surrogate-assisted evolutionary computation often is used for reducing the computational time of evaluation of individuals' fitness value. When the target of the application is real, we need complex computer simulations or real experiments to calculate a fitness value. Table 1 shows the relationship between the evaluation method, resource efficiency, and the fidelity of fitness.

Table 1. The relationship between the evaluation method, resource efficiency, and the fidelity of fitness.

Evaluation Method	Resource Efficiency	Fidelity of Fitness
Experiment	Low	High
Simluation	Middle	Middle
Model	High	Low

This paper utilizes the blockchain mechanism for the population-based optimization system to make a trust management system. We adopt evolutionary computation as a reference model. By using blockchain, we can implement it without a central authority. In the system, all interactions are reviewed and get feedback, and the feedback is used to calculate the trust score.

2   Usecases of Blockchain in Evolutionary Computation

A blockchain [10] is a list of records, called blocks, linked together using cryptography. Each block contains a cryptographic hash of the previous block, a timestamp, and transaction data. Figure 1 and Fig. 2 show examples of the usage of blockchain in evolutionary computation.

When blockchains are used as a distributed ledger, they are usually managed by a peer-to-peer network and conform to protocols for inter-node communication and verification of new blocks. Once a block's data has been recorded, it cannot be changed retroactively without changing all subsequent blocks. For this reason, blockchain is considered secure by design and is an example of a decentralized computing system with high Byzantine fault tolerance. These make decentralized consensus a key concept in the blockchain. We use blockchain as a tool of maintaining trust.

Bitcoin [10] and Ethereum [11] are two of the most popular blockchains. While Bitcoin is a book of currency, Ethereum is a book of programs. In Ethereum, any computer program can be put on the ledger, which has attracted worldwide attention as it enables smart contracts, decentralized finance, and decentralized exchanges. Therefore, this paper proposes utilizing blockchain technologies but is not specific to Ethereum.

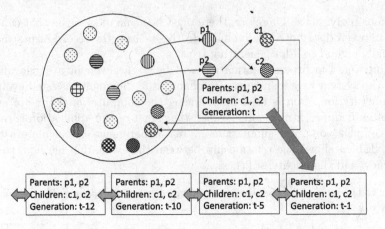

Fig. 1. The usage of blockchain in evolutionary computation (1).

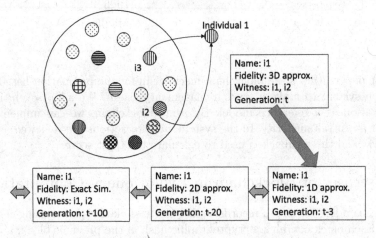

Fig. 2. The usage of blockchain in evolutionary computation (2).

Ethereum is a platform for building decentralized applications and smart contracts and is the generic name of a related open-source software project being developed by the Ethereum Project. Ether is used as the internal currency required to use Ethereum. Ethereum is designed as a general-purpose computer and can run a virtual machine.

There are two consensus algorithms for Ethereum: one is for Proof of Work (POW), called "Ethash," and the other is for Proof of Stake (POS), called "Casper".

3   Trust in Evolutionary Computation with Blockchain

This paper concerns the reliability of each individual's information in distributed evolutionary computation. As noted in Sect. 1, the information may not be reliable in a distributed environment for some reason. For example, when the computation is carried over the distributed machines, some machines may work differently from the rest by failure or malicious action. Moreover, the fitness information will be vague even in a single machine when the system uses a surrogate mechanism. Therefore, we have to estimate how the other individual can be trusted.

Let us assume individuals in evolutionary computation. An individual wants to know the fitness value of other individuals to produce good offspring. In usual evolutionary computation, the fitness value is assumed to be correct. However, we assume distributed environment. In this case, the individual has to estimate the fitness through the record of other individuals' actions. The individual has to decide which individual to trust. The fitness value provided by different individuals may differ. For instance, one may offer a quick answer at a lower quality, while another may be slow but accurate.

While the individual will be confident of the validity of their previous interactions with other individuals, they cannot rely on their knowledge to provide certainty in other individuals' interactions. We can solve this problem by storing the verified feedback of the record of interaction on the blockchain. Such feedback can be accessed by any trust provider, which offers trust scores as a service. When we use blockchain, the information is available to all parties. This means that the information and trust scoring mechanisms have the following properties: Universal, Transparent, and Verifiable. As an added benefit, the integration of blockchain into the system enables payment for resource access, including trust score estimation.

We take a quantitative approach to reason about trust, using the information which is built from the feedback of interaction between individuals. The trust calculation is done by direct experiences by aggregating individual feedback scores to form an overall individual opinion about the quality of interaction or reliability of other individuals. Sometimes, direct experience may not be possible when no interaction may have occurred between individuals. In this case, the individual would rely on third-person's information to infer information from other individuals.

4   System Architecture

Figure 3 shows the architecture of our proposed system for evolutionary computation. This system is inspired by Pal's work [12].

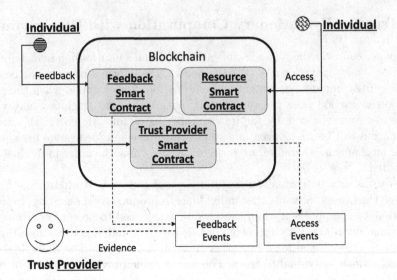

Fig. 3. The system architecture for evolutionary computation incorporating trust in uncertain environments.

This architecture has three main components: individuals, trust providers, and smart contracts. In the system, individuals can be both information providers and consumers. Individuals can store information, access a resource, deploy smart contracts, and communicate with one another. Trust providers maintain trust scores. Smart contacts are collections of code and data used to execute agreements between two individuals and stored on a blockchain. We use three types of smart contracts:

- Resource smart contract: that handles access to a resource,
- Feedback smart contract: that handles the reviews submitted by the individuals,
- Trust provider's smart contract: that helps the trust providers maintain trust scores.

The system is composed of a public blockchain that keeps track of all delegated access rights, consumer interactions, and consumer feedback directly linked to one consumer interaction.

The smart contract handles reviews submitted by individuals in the system. It receives a review rating and ensures that the review is linked to interaction. It ensures that a submitted review has the following parts:

- Address of the individual that submits the review,
- Details of the interaction reviewed, and
- A review rating.

The correctness of the system can be verified by all individuals interacting with the public blockchain.

The trust provider is responsible for the trust scoring functions and making the output available to the individuals for some access fee. The trust provider complements its soundness by choosing a scoring mechanism and an evidence selection to implement. Figure 4 shows the relationship between interactions, feedbacks, and evidence.

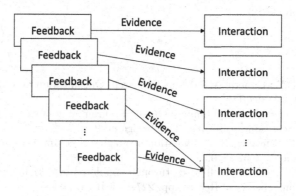

Fig. 4. The relationship between interactions, feedbacks, and evidences.

The communication between the components of the system proceeds as follows:

1. When an individual wants to check the information of other individuals, he asks the trust provider.
2. The trust provider retrieves a pre-computed score or performs an on-demand trust score calculation.
3. Once the resource has been used an event will be generated on the blockchain.
4. The trust provider will be notified of the new resource access since the event is broadcast on the public chain.
5. The trust providers will then update the feedback smart contract on the blockchain to update the feedback state.
6. If the individual is willing, they can leave feedback for that resource.

We can calculate the trust score by the following equation:

$$\sigma(A) = \sum_l \mu(\alpha_l) \prod_k \omega(i_k, x_{kl}) \tag{1}$$

where, A is a set of interactions, μ is a scoring mechanism, and ω is evidence selection.

5   Conclusion

This paper proposed a framework for trust systems for evolutionary computation where the record of interactions backs up evidence. The blockchain mechanism is utilized in the population-based optimization system to introduce a trust management system. By using blockchain, we can implement it without a central authority. In the system, all interactions are reviewed and get feedback, and the feedback is used to calculate the trust score. We consider several scoring methods for this type of system, and averaging approach is simple yet powerful. In future works, we will implement the framework using Ethereum, and a feasibility study should be conducted.

References

1. Goldberg, D.E.: Genetic Algorithms in Search, Optimization and Machine Learning. Addison-Wesley (1989)
2. Koza, J.R.: Genetic Programming, On the Programming of Computers by Means of Natural Selection. MIT Press, Cambridge (1992)
3. Beyer, H.G., Schwefel, H.P.: Evolution strategies: a comprehensive introduction. Nat. Comput. **1**, 3–52 (2002)
4. Fogel, D.B.: Artificial intelligence through simulated evolution. In: Evolutionary Computation: The Fossil Record, pp. 227–296. IEEE (1998)
5. Bonyadi, M.R., Michalewicz, Z.: Particle swarm optimization for single objective continuous space problems: a review. Evol. Comput. **25**(1), 1–54 (2017)
6. Dorigo, M., Birattari, M., Stutzle, T.: Ant colony optimization. IEEE Comput. Intell. Mag. **1**(4), 28–39 (2006)
7. Dasgupta, D. (ed.): Artificial Immune Systems and Their Applications. Springer, Berlin (1999). https://doi.org/10.1007/978-3-642-59901-9
8. Lamport, L., Shostak, R., Pease, M.: The Byzantine generals problem. ACM Trans. Program. Lang. Syst. **4**(3), 382–401 (1982)
9. Jin, Y.: Surrogate-assisted evolutionary computation: recent advances and future challenges. Swarm Evol. Comput. **1**(2), 61–70 (2011)
10. Brotsis, S., Limniotis, K., Bendiab, G., Kolokotronis, N., Shiaeles, S.: On the suitability of blockchain platforms for IoT applications: Architectures, security, privacy, and performance. Comput. Netw. **191**, 108005 (2021)
11. Ethereum Project. https://ethereum.org/. Accessed 10 July 2022
12. Pal, S., Hill, A., Rabehaja, T., Hitchens, M.: A blockchain-based trust management framework with verifiable interactions. Comput. Netw. **200**, 108506 (2021)

Efficient Inductive Logic Programming Based on Particle Swarm Optimization

Kyosuke Obara[1]([✉]), Munehiro Takimoto[1], Tsutomu Kumazawa[2],
and Yasushi Kambayashi[3]

[1] Department of Information Sciences, Tokyo University of Science, Chiba, Japan
6322510@ed.tus.ac.jp, mune@rs.tus.ac.jp
[2] Software Research Associates, Inc. Toshima-ku, Tokyo, Japan
kumazawa@sra.co.jp
[3] Department of Computer and Information Engineering,
Nippon Institute of Technology, Saitama, Japan
yasushi@nit.ac.jp

Abstract. Inductive Logic Programming (ILP) is an inductive reasoning method based on the first-order predicative logic. This technology is widely used for data mining using symbolic artificial intelligence. ILP searches for a suitable hypothesis that covers positive examples and uncovers negative examples. The searching process requires a lot of execution cost to interpret many given examples for practical problems. In this paper, we propose a new hypothesis search method using particle swarm optimization (PSO). PSO is a meta-heuristic algorithm based on behaviors of particles. In our approach, each particle repeatedly moves from a hypothesis to another hypothesis within a hypothesis space. At that time, some hypotheses are refined based on the value returned by a predefined evaluation function. Since PSO just searches a part of the hypothesis space, it contributes to the speed up of the execution of ILP. In order to demonstrate the effectiveness of our method, we have implemented it on Progol that is one of the ILP systems [6], and then we conducted numerical experiments. The results showed that our method reduced the hypothesis search time compared to another conventional Progol.

Keywords: Inductive logic programming · Particle swarm optimization · Progol

1 Introduction

Finding a general theory from concrete examples has been the mainstream of scientific world. Data mining is a recent popular technique for this purpose. A scientist who is engaging in data mining is called a data scientist, and it is a popular occupation now. The spread of machine learning including deep learning has contributed to a lot of data mining through generating structured data

Y. Kambayashi et al. (Eds.): AICON 2022, LNICST 477, pp. 151–158, 2023.
https://doi.org/10.1007/978-3-031-29126-5_13

such as data bases from unstructured data such as images and sounds. On the other hand, data scientists have not sufficiently investigated the relations among structured data due to the nature of machine learning. To extract knowledge in the structured data from a single database or inter-related multiple databases, Inductive Logic Programing (ILP) [5] is known to be useful. Therefore, ILP is expected to be effective for data mining. ILP is an inductive reasoning methodology based on the first-order predicate logic. It tries to induce a general theory from specific examples. ILP searches for a simple hypothesis that covers positive examples and uncovers negative examples based on background knowledge. ILP generates the hypothesis candidates through generalizing positive examples, and then it verifies each candidate through covering positive examples and uncovering negative examples. ILP deals with the hypothesis as rules of the first-order predicate logic. A hypothesis is added to background knowledge, so that the background knowledge is extended. If all the examples with the same predicate as the hypothesis are deduced from the extended background knowledge, we can confirm that the induced hypothesis is valid. This validation process is a simple deductive reasoning practiced in the standard logic programming, and it shows that the examples are correct or incorrect.

Thus, when we pursue the explainable artificial intelligence, ILP is a strong data mining tool. It implements the explainable symbolic artificial intelligence. On the other hand, ILP tends to require a lot of execution time in practical cases. We can reduce the execution cost by parallelizing covering examples or searching hypotheses. However, parallelization requires other computational resources, and limits the effectiveness of such approaches. In this paper, we propose a method efficiently detecting a hypothesis using Particle Swarm Optimization (PSO) [4]. We call our method PSOProgol. It stands for a PSO based Progol.

PSO is a meta-heuristic algorithm inspired by the behavior of birds and fishes. The meta-heuristic algorithms can find semi-optimal solutions in the huge search space with less time and memory than exhaustive methods can do. As an approach similar to our method, i.e. ILP with meta-heuristic, Ant-FOIL has been proposed [12]. Ant-FOIL is an ILP system built on the top of FOIL [11] and it takes advantages of the ant colony optimization (ACO). FOIL is an ILP system based on a downward refinement operator. Refinement operators are frequently used in ILP. ACO is a meta-heuristic algorithm inspired by behaviors of ants [2]. Ant-FOIL contributes to improving predictive accuracy but not its performance. It has the same limitation as the original FOIL; it uses the base atoms as its available background knowledge as the original FOIL does. We have built a new ILP system on top of Progol. Progol can use any Horn clause as background knowledge [6]. In terms of meta-heuristic algorithms, PSO is often used to find the location of a target when only the distance to the target is known, while ACO is often used to find the shortest path when the target location and distance to it are known. Therefore, we adopt PSO to Progol. When we have applied PSOProgol to three public problems, we have observed that the bigger the problems we have to tackle, the more efficiency we can get to obtain hypotheses compared to the conventional Progol.

The rest of this paper is organized as follows. Section 2 describes a brief introduction to Progol as a representation system of ILP systems, and Sect. 3 describes PSO. Section 4 gives a detailed description of our proposed method. Section 5 presents our experimental results, and Sect. 6 gives conclusions and future work.

2 Progol

Figure 1 shows the outline of Progol's learning algorithm [6]. B is a set of the background knowledge, E is a set of positive examples, and H is a set of hypotheses. Most Specific Hypothesis (MSH) is a hypothesis that has all possible literals, and all the literals of each generated hypothesis candidate construct a subset of ones of the MSH. MSH is generated by generalizing each positive examples (line 2 in Fig. 1). Progol generates hypothesis candidates by adding some literals in MSH to an empty clause. What hypotheses are generated depends on which literals are added to the basic candidate. Focusing on the relation between the base candidate and newly generated candidate, we can represent the hypothesis space as a directed acyclic graph (DAG), as shown in Fig. 2. The process of generating a more specific hypothesis candidate through adding some literals to the base candidate is called refinement. In the refinement, selecting which hypothesis to refine affects accuracy and efficiency of the search. Progol tries to find the simplest hypothesis, which covers all the positive examples and covers as few negative examples as possible, in the top-down direction in the DAG structure while checking each candidate with an evaluation function. Notice that hypothesis candidate is not as specific as MSH, which is the bottom of the DAG structure. Once a suitable hypothesis is found (line 3), it is added to the background knowledge (line 4), and the positive examples covered by it are eliminated from the positive examples to generalize the hypothesis (lines 5 and 6). Thus, lines 1–7 are repeated until the set of positive examples for generalization becomes an empty set (line 1). Finally, the set B returned in line 1 becomes the background knowledge with the hypothesis covering all the positive examples.

Progol's evaluation function f is expressed by the following equation:

$$f = p - (n + c + h) \tag{1}$$

Each variable is defined as follows. p is the number of positive examples covered by the candidate hypothesis and n is the number of negative examples covered by the candidate hypothesis. c is the number of literals in the hypothesis body part, and h is the minimum number of the literals that should be added to complete the input-output relationships of the candidate hypothesis. All the hypotheses with the complete input-output relationships have the corresponding input and output variables in the head literal. They have either the same input and output variables in the head or chained ones in the body of the hypothesis. We call the length of the chain the length of the hypothesis. Thus, h represents the distance to the target hypothesis.

```
1: if E = ∅, return B
2: Generate MSH from the beginning e of E.
3: A*-like search algorithm generates H.
4: B ← B ∪ H
5: E' ← {e' :e' ∈ E and B implies e'}
6: E ← E\E'
7: go to 1
```

Fig. 1. Progol Algorithm

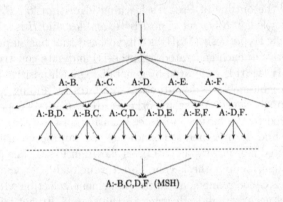

Fig. 2. Progol's Hypothesis Space

3   Particle Swarm Optimization

In PSO, multiple particles search for semi-optimal solutions while moving in a given search space. Each particle i has information on its position x_i, velocity v_i, and the local best position $pBest_i$ with the highest evaluation value for the particle. In addition, particles share the global best position $gBest$ with the highest evaluation value in the entire swarm. The i-th particle changes its velocity vector with the values of $pBest_i$ and $gBest$. As shown in Fig. 3, the position at time $(t + 1)$ is closer to the direction of $pBest_i$ and $gBest$ than the position at time t. PSO tries to avoid the local maxima through considering not only $gBest$ but also $pBest_i$. The velocity and position of each particle are determined by the following formulae:

$$v_i = w \cdot v_i + c_1 \cdot rand_1 \cdot (pBest_i - x_i) + c_2 \cdot rand_2 \cdot (gBest - x_i) \quad (2)$$

$$x_i = x_i + v_i \quad (3)$$

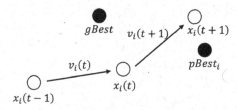

Fig. 3. Particle Movement

The velocity of each particle is updated through Eq. (2) at each step. Values $rand_1$ and $rand_2$ are randomly decided at each step respectively. Coefficients w, c_1 and c_2 are empirically determined. Once the velocity is updated, the position of the particle is updated through Eq. (3).

4   PSO Based Progol

Original Progol performs hypothesis search by A*-like algorithm. This algorithm mimics the A* algorithm but efficiently finds the optimal solution. It is a kind of heuristics sacrificing strict optimality in order to get efficiency. Thus, although the search strategy of Progol aims at efficiently finding a solution, it still takes long time in some practical cases. In order to mitigate this problem, PSOProgol uses PSO for its hypothetical search. PSO has an advantage for searching in a huge hypothesis space. In PSOProgol, a particle swarm moves through the hypotheses in the search space and refines the hypothesis with the best evaluation value. Since Progol tries to maximize the evaluation function (1), the ILP problem can be considered as the optimization problem that maximizes the value of (1). Thus, PSOProgol employs the function (1) as its fitness function and tries to maximize its value. Therefore, $pBest_i$ and $gBest$ can be related to Progol's evaluation function, and the velocity and position of the particles can be updated based on the evaluation of the function. The depth of MSH can be computed beforehand and PSOProgol assigns this depth as the dimension of position vectors. Note that the precomputation of the maximum depth is the main reason why PSO is suitable with ILP. Also, in order to relate the ILP hypothesis space to PSO search space, each hypothesis on a path from the root to MSH must be related to each component of a position vector in the PSO search space in accordance with the manner of [3]. The relation between paths in the hypothesis space and positions in the PSO search space is shown in Fig. 4. Each path on the DAG in Fig. 4 can be represented by a sequence of indices that are labeled on edges in the figure. The first component of the position vector represents the depth of the hypothesis, and the vector's dimension is "The depth of MSH + 1". The position vectors' components that do not indicate any edge indices are initialzed to 0. For example, the coordinate (2,1,2,0,...,0) corresponds to the hypothesis "A:-C" and the coordinate (3,1,1,2,0,... 0) corresponds to the hypothesis "A:-B,D".

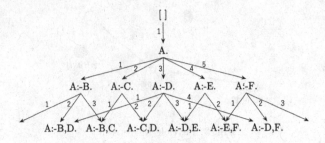

Fig. 4. The hypothesis space with paths

Figure 5 shows the algorithm of PSOProgol. First, initialize the particle swarm(line 1 in Fig. 5). The initial positions of all particles are the coordinates of the hypothesis "[]" and the initial velocity is 0. Next, the positions and velocities are updated according to Eq. (2) and (3) (line 2). The hypothesis corresponding to each particle's position is refined and the generated hypothesis is added to the hypothesis space(line 3). The $pBest_i$ and $gBest$ are updated based on the evaluated value of the hypothesis corresponding to the position of each particle after its movement(line 4 and 5). The above process is repeated until the termination condition is met. The termination condition is that the positive example set is empty, as in Progol.

```
1 Initialize the position and velocity of each particle.
2 Update the position and velocity of each particle.
3 Refine the hypothesis of the node to which each particle is moving
    and add it to the hypothesis space.
4 Update the pBest
5 Update the gBest
6 If termination conditions are met, output gBest and exit.
7 Repeat steps 3 through 6.
```

Fig. 5. Algorithm of PSOProgol

5 Experiments

In order to demonstrate the effectiveness of our approach, we have implemented PSOProgol in OCaml 5.0.0. We then conducted numerical experiments and evaluated it's execution time and compared the corresponding values to the conventional Progol's for three datasets, Grammar, Animals and Append [8]. These are public-domain benchmark datasets provided by the Progol developers. Grammar checks whether a given English sentence is grammatically correct or not, Animals classifies a given animal, and Append concatenates two lists. We took the average of 30 experiments for each dataset because both Progol and PSOProgol employ randomized approaches. In Progol, negative examples are automatically generated based on stochastic logic programs [7]. In PSOProgol, Formula (2) contains random numbers. The parameters of the PSO were set as per Table 1. These values were determined through several preliminary experiments. Since the initial position of all particles is set to the most general and empty hypothesis, the value of w was set to a larger value of 1.5 so that they disperse more quickly. We have conducted experiments on Apple M1 with MacOS Monterey version 12.4 and 8 GB memory.

As shown in the Fig. 6, conventional Progol was a little faster than PSOProgol in Append, but in Grammar and Animals, PSOProgol was faster than conventional one.

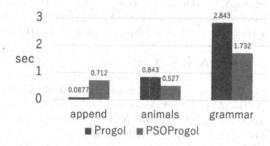

Fig. 6. Execution time for each problem

Table 1. Parameters of PSOProgol

Parameter	Value
w	1.5
c_1	1
c_2	1
Maximum Depth	Depth of MSH
Number of Particles	45

While PSOProgol is less efficient for small hypothesis spaces such as Append because of the time it takes to move multiple particles and the random numbers involved, it is more efficient in huge hypothesis spaces such as Grammar and Animals as well as PSO. Regarding accuracy, the hypotheses generated by Progol and PSOProgol were identical. The experiments show that PSOProgol becomes faster than Progol in hypothesis search as the size of the hypothesis space increases and has an advantage in practical cases.

6   Conclusions and Future Work

We have proposed a new ILP system PSOProgol that combines a heuristic algorithm PSO and a broadly descriptive algorithm Progol. Through the numerical experiments, we have observed that PSOProgol is faster than conventional

Progol when the hypothesis space enlarges. Therefore, the proposed method is effective in data mining, where the data may be huge and faster execution speed is required. As future work, we plan to extend PSOProgol using parallel and distributed processing [1,9,10]. Specifically, further speed-up can be expected by dividing the search space and separating particles into multiple groups.

References

1. Algahtani, E., Kazakov, D.: GPU-accelerated hypothesis cover set testing for learning in logic. In: Riguzzi, F., Bellodi, E., Zese, R. (eds.) ILP Up-and-Coming/Short Papers. CEUR Workshop Proceedings, vol. 2206, pp. 6–20. CEUR-WS.org (2018)
2. Dorigo, M., Stuetzle, T.: Ant Colony Optimization. The MIT Press, Cambridge (2004)
3. Ferreira, M., Chicano, F., Alba, E., Gómez-Pulido, J.A.: Detecting protocol errors using particle swarm optimization with Java pathfinder. In: Smari, W.W. (ed.) Proceedings of the High Performance Computing & Simulation Conference (2008)
4. Kennedy, J., Eberhart, R.: Particle swarm optimization. In: Proceedings of ICNN'95 - International Conference on Neural Networks, vol. 4, pp. 1942–1948 (1995). https://doi.org/10.1109/ICNN.1995.488968
5. Muggleton, S.: Inductive logic programming. New Gener. Comput. **8**, 295–318 (1991)
6. Muggleton, S.: Inverse entailment and progol. New Gener. Comput. Spec. Issue Induct. Logic Program. **13**(3–4), 245–286 (1995). https://citeseer.nj.nec.com/muggleton95inverse.html
7. Muggleton, S.: Stochastic logic programs (1996)
8. Muggleton, S.: Progol (2003). https://www.doc.ic.ac.uk/shm/progol.html
9. Nishiyama, H., Ohwada, H.: Parallel inductive logic programming system for superlinear speedup. In: Lachiche, N., Vrain, C. (eds.) ILP 2017. LNCS (LNAI), vol. 10759, pp. 112–123. Springer, Cham (2018). https://doi.org/10.1007/978-3-319-78090-0_8
10. Ohwada, H., Nishiyama, H., Mizoguchi, F.: Concurrent execution of optimal hypothesis search for inverse entailment. In: Cussens, J., Frisch, A. (eds.) ILP 2000. LNCS (LNAI), vol. 1866, pp. 165–173. Springer, Heidelberg (2000). https://doi.org/10.1007/3-540-44960-4_10
11. Quinlan, J.R.: Learning logical definitions from relations. Mach. Learn. **5**, 239–266 (2004)
12. Yan, C.: Ant-FOIL: integrating ant colony system and FOIL. In: 2015 7th International Conference on Intelligent Human-Machine Systems and Cybernetics, vol. 1, pp. 559–562 (2015). https://doi.org/10.1109/IHMSC.2015.20

Author Index

Y. Kambayashi et al. (Eds.): AICON 2022, LNICST 477, p. 159, 2023.
https://doi.org/10.1007/978-3-031-29126-5

Printed in the United States
by Baker & Taylor Publisher Services